1812

Rediscovering Chesapeake Bay's
Forgotten War

DAVID HEALEY

*To Morgan
Enjoy the rediscovery!*

[signature]

BellaRosaBooks

1812: Rediscovering Chesapeake Bay's Forgotten War
ISBN 0-9747685-2-9

For more information contact
Bella Rosa Books, P.O. Box 4251 CRS, Rock Hill, SC 29732.
Or online at www.bellarosabooks.com

First Printing: May 2005

Library of Congress Control Number: 200592618

Printed in the United States of America on acid-free paper.

Cover photograph: Jerome Bird, Pride of Baltimore, Inc.
Book design by Bella Rosa Books

BellaRosaBooks and logo are trademarks of Bella Rosa Books

"My countrymen, we hold a rich deposit in trust for ourselves and for all our brethren of mankind. It is the fire of Liberty. If it becomes extinguished, our darkened land will cast a mournful shadow over the nations. If it lives, its blaze will enlighten and gladden the whole earth."

—*Francis Scott Key*, speaking at a Fourth of July celebration in Washington

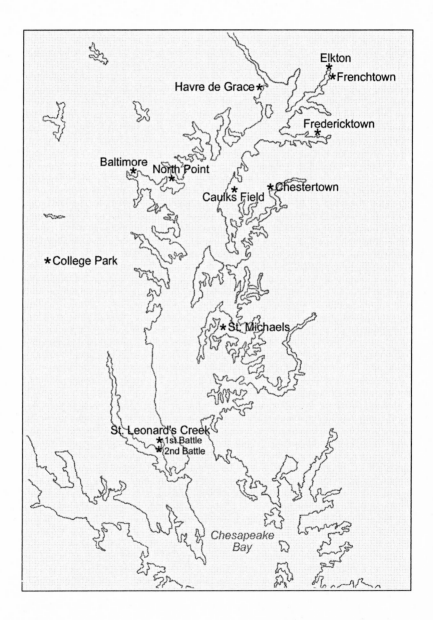

Elkton
*
*Frenchtown

Havre de Grace*

Fredericktown
*

Baltimore   North Point
*   *

Caulks Field   *Chestertown
*

*College Park

*St. Michaels

St. Leonard's Creek
*1st Battle
*2nd Battle

Chesapeake
Bay

Contents

Introduction

One of my favorite anecdotes about the War of 1812 on Chesapeake Bay comes from the town of St. Michaels. This old shipbuilding center on the Miles River was the target of the Royal Navy on the night of August 10, 1813. As British ships prepared to bombard St. Michaels, residents hatched a plan to save their town. They hung dozens of lanterns from the masts of ships in the harbor and from tall trees, then snuffed all other lights in town. When the British opened fire, aiming for the lights, the cannonballs flew high above the houses. The Royal Navy sailed away that night and St. Michaels became known as "The Town that Fooled the British."

The War of 1812 is rich with stories like that, about how clever or determined Marylanders fought back against a powerful foreign military foe that had invaded their homeland. More often than not, the British weren't so easily fooled or defeated. Waterfront towns and farms up and down the Chesapeake Bay were looted and burned. Even the city of Washington would be destroyed by the invaders. The War of 1812 has a fiery history of burning and pillaging, heroism and incompetence, 1800s-era spin doctors and overlooked importance.

Most of the information in this book relies on what William Warner, Pulitzer Prize-winning author of *Beautiful Swimmers: Watermen, Crabs and the Chesapeake Bay*, would have called "rack of eye and yarning." In other words, much of the research consisted of tramping around historical sites and re-enactments, soaking up history and talking with others eager to share their love of the past.

Along the way I made some wonderful rediscoveries of out-of-the-way places and fascinating people. I came across a man who makes his living portraying President James Madison, War of 1812 re-enactors, archaeologists and dendrochronologists, lonely country graveyards and fanatics for obscure local history.

Except for a five-hour drive to Montpelier in Virginia and a weekend trip to southern Maryland, my forays into history were usually limited to how far I could get on a Saturday or Sunday, often with two young children in the back of the car and a patient wife navigating with a map of Maryland spread across the dashboard. When it comes to the War of 1812 on Chesapeake Bay, that's about as far as you have to go.

Chapter by chapter, I began to write about the Chesapeake Bay's forgotten war. The book that follows is a way of sharing this rediscovery of the War of 1812. The focus here is on the War of 1812 in the Chesapeake Bay region rather than the Great Lakes campaign and invasion of Canada or the spectacular battle of New Orleans. The places mentioned are all in Maryland unless otherwise noted. I hope that you get an opportunity to visit some of these historical locations and that you enjoy the journey as much as I have.

Notes and Acknowledgments

Everyone who took time to talk about 1812 had a special part in this project. I am thankful to them all and hope that in some small way this book will rekindle more interest in the War of 1812.

Two exceptional individuals should be mentioned here. Michael Dixon, president of Historic Elk Landing Foundation, showed constant interest in this project and was always offering tips on where to run down information. His enthusiasm for history knows no bounds.

Also, a special thanks to Stan Quick, the expert on the battle of Caulk's Field who lent so much of his time taking me on a tour of the site as well as reading the chapter on Caulk's Field and offering his suggestions. He is writing a history of 1812 on the Chesapeake Bay and we will all be lucky indeed to read it one day.

What quickly becomes apparent when researching 1812 is that there are very few books about this conflict, especially when compared to the number written about the Civil War. There are books on almost every Civil War topic imaginable, from cookbooks to technical manuals on weapons and strategy to collected letters and journals. There are whole bookstores that sell nothing but Civil War titles. By comparison, you would be hard-pressed to fill a single bookshelf with volumes about 1812.

Most valuable among the handful of 1812 books were *Terror on the Chesapeake* by Christopher T. George and

The War of 1812 by Harry Coles. George's book was a constant reference for looking up dates and specifics about the Chesapeake Bay campaign. Coles' book provides an excellent and interesting overview of the entire war with details on the Chesapeake Bay. Also, Donald Shomette's book *Lost Towns of Tidewater Maryland* provided some insight into the attack on Georgetown and Kitty Knight's dark side.

Several articles also were helpful, especially those published in the *Cecil Whig* (Cecil County) and *The Sun* (Baltimore). Established in 1841, the *Cecil Whig* has given thorough coverage to 1812 history and discoveries on the Eastern Shore of Maryland. *The Sun* has in recent years provided a great deal of coverage about the Flag House in Baltimore, Fort McHenry, the national anthem and the Star-Spangled Banner flag. Many of these articles were in the archives of the Historical Society of Cecil County.

The Internet was a valuable tool in obtaining information about the War of 1812. The *Pride of Baltimore II* website is very helpful to anyone interested in Baltimore's maritime history. The James Madison Center at James Madison University website also offers a tremendous online archive of information relating to the fourth president.

Special appreciation is due to Bella Rosa Books and Rod Hunter, who not only published the book, but also offered much helpful editorial advice. His sharp-eyed copyeditors made sense of jumbled sentences and kept the book pointed in the right direction. Similar appreciation is owed to the friends who read parts of the manuscript and offered their suggestions.

Finally, a special thanks to my wife, Joanne. She has the courage of Kitty Knight and the level-headedness of Mary Young Pickersgill and the dazzle of Dolley Madison. Her tireless support made this book possible. She's the best.

1

The Second War of Independence
An upstart nation fights for survival

On a January day in 1815, the full might of the British Empire faced a ragtag army of Americans across a muddy field outside the city of New Orleans. The simple fact that the British were there was testimony to their determination and capacity for making war. They had carried men, supplies and massive cannons through the swamps of Louisiana in what was an incredible feat of military logistics. Now, the British in their red coats were lined in orderly rows awaiting the signal to attack.

In that moment, the fate of the young United States appeared to hang on the outcome of the battle. What the British had not been able to finish thirty years before during the American Revolution, they were determined to do now. This fight would settle, once and for all, the future of the upstart democracy. Would it be a tiny, seacoast nation boxed in by the new British territories or would the United States expand across a continent?

The Americans were about to meet an army that had conquered India and defeated Napoleon. The veteran officers of European battlefields confidently believed they would scatter the American army made up of farmers, pioneers, pirates, Creoles, mulattos and former slaves, then advance up the Mississippi River to split the United States neatly in two.

Given the way the war had gone so far in America, their confidence was justified.

A rocket crawled into the winter sky. From the American lines, General Andrew Jackson realized it was the signal for the attack to begin. The neat rows of British troops advanced toward the Americans.

Instead of a British victory, it was a slaughter. In the next forty-five minutes, the British army suffered nearly 3000 men killed, captured or wounded as they attacked the American fortifications. The Americans lost roughly six killed and seven wounded.

In one of history's great ironies, this final battle took place after the war was already over. Two weeks earlier in Europe, British and United States negotiators had signed the Treaty of Ghent, bringing the war to an end. In those days news could only travel as swift as the fastest ship, and that wasn't soon enough to spare the lives of so many British soldiers. If the British had won the battle, they might have ignored the treaty. American victories at New Orleans and Baltimore had sealed the treaty more effectively than mere signatures.

Mention the War of 1812 and most Americans will know it took place in . . . well, 1812. They don't know it's the year America went to war for the second time with the British, launching a conflict that would bring about the burning of the White House and United States Capitol, the writing of the national anthem and even the legend of Uncle Sam.

Considering that the last battle came after the treaty ending the war, it is perhaps fitting that the first battle came before war was officially declared on June 19, 1812. In 1807, a sea battle on Chesapeake Bay pitted the *HMS Leopard* against the *USS Chesapeake*. The Americans suffered an embarrassing loss when their ship was caught unprepared and was quickly defeated. It was a pattern that would be repeated in land battles throughout the coming war as American generals, who had no business being on a battlefield, took on crack British troops.

Later in the war, Chesapeake Bay would once again be the setting for a major clash between British and American forces. This time, it would be the Royal Navy's turn to suffer embarrassment at Fort McHenry during the Battle of Baltimore.

"At this time our morning gun was fired," wrote Issac Munroe, one of the fort's defenders, "the flag was hoisted, Yankee Doodle played, and we all appeared in full view of a formidable and mortified enemy, who calculated upon our surrender in twenty minutes after the commencement of the action."

Two main grievances lay at the heart of American animosity toward Great Britain. The young United States was already outgrowing its coastal boundaries and expanding westward. The Lewis and Clark expedition encouraged by President Thomas Jefferson in 1803 had ventured into the continent beyond the Appalachian Mountains and the Mississippi River.

Britain, too, had seen the possibilities of this vast land and already controlled a huge amount of territory in its Canadian provinces. Rather than leave well enough alone, the British encouraged American Indians in their fight against white settlers moving westward from the original United States. Those who had lost their farms or loved ones to Indian raids were no friends of the British.

Meanwhile, on the East Coast, the British were restricting American trade, completely ignoring the fact that the United States was a sovereign nation. As far as the British were concerned, it was as if the United States of America did not exist, and if it did, it was only an upstart nation and a minor nuisance.

On the high seas, the British stopped American vessels, boarded them, and took away sailors to work their own Royal Navy ships. The British claimed the American sailors were actually deserters from His Majesty's vessels. On occasion there were deserters, but usually the sailors the British scooped up were American citizens. The British also refused to recognize that a man born in Ireland or England or Scotland could become an American citizen. The British view was that once a subject of the king, always a subject of the king. The Royal Navy was running roughshod over American ships in a perfect case of "might makes right" and there was little the American government could do about it.

No amount of complaining through diplomatic channels seemed to do any good. The United States invoked a reverse trade embargo intended to punish the British, but which only bankrupted American merchants. The British were too preoccupied with fighting Napoleon to pay much attention. In any case, there wasn't any reason to worry about what Americans thought. Britain had nothing to fear from a young United States that lacked any real economic or military clout.

At the middle of this maelstrom was President James "Jemmy" Madison. He was just the fourth president of what was then the world's only democracy. Madison took office on the heels of George Washington, John Adams and Thomas Jefferson.

Talk about a tough act to follow. Madison was overshadowed by these fellow Founding Fathers. It did not help that Madison was a small man and his legendary colleagues literally towered over him.

Madison is probably best known to most Americans as the "Father of the Constitution." He was possibly the most intellectual president, more brilliant in many respects than

Jefferson. Madison, however, carried modesty to an extreme. He strove to be self-effacing, and history ultimately granted him the wish of obscurity.

In many ways, Madison was the ultimate public servant. He dedicated his life to founding and nurturing the young nation. As president he was neither charismatic nor decisive. Madison might have been a master politician, but he made a better legislator than a chief executive. For all his accomplishments, he was a humble man who lacked the natural spark of leadership.

Somewhat unfairly, the political enemies of his administration would come to call the War of 1812 "Mr. Madison's War." Besieged on all sides by demands for war in the face of continuing British outrages, Madison had little choice but to take action and request that Congress issue a declaration of war. Unlike the hawks surrounding him, Madison understood that the United States was ill-prepared to fight the British. His good friend Thomas Jefferson, ever suspicious of a strong central government, shrank the young nation's military as a cost-saving measure during his own presidency.

When the United States went to war it had only a few ships to confront the Royal Navy's huge fleet and just a few thousand regular army soldiers. On paper the vast citizen-army empowered by the Second Amendment and known as the militia looked impressive. Theoretically, hundreds of thousands of armed men stood ready to come to the defense of their nation. Many of those men were husbands, fathers, farmers and merchants first and foremost, but only half-hearted soldiers. They had no military training and their weapons were usually fowling pieces better suited to shooting ducks than Redcoats.

The war got off to a bad start. Most of the generals were

tired and timid old veterans of the Revolution. They had served their country well in the past. With youthful vigor gone, they were unprepared to lead troops into battle thirty years later.

The strategy was as poor as the leadership. The American plan to invade Canada early in the war was a complete failure. There were stunning military losses and terrible defeats. Instead of enthusiastically joining the United States as American war hawks had predicted, Canadians fought to defend their homeland. Americans had badly miscalculated the Canadian situation, and found that the few Redcoats posted to defend Canada were more than enough to trounce American militia.

Indian wars on the frontier made matters worse. Today we think of most battles with American Indians taking place out West—such as General Custer's ill-fated battle of the Little Big Horn. In 1812 the frontier was much closer, stretching from Wisconsin down through Ohio and into Louisiana. The Indian nations of this frontier united under a charismatic Shawnee war leader named Tecumseh. With British supplies of arms and ammunition, Tecumseh set about halting the westward expansion of the United States.

In the Chesapeake Bay region, American defenses were quickly outgunned and overwhelmed by the more powerful Royal Navy ships. The entire Chesapeake Bay became an "English Pond" controlled by His Majesty's ships. By 1813, British amphibious forces were raiding waterfront towns and plantations at will in Maryland and Virginia. American militia forces on land tried to fight back, but the hit-and-run tactics of the British made this difficult. When a telltale plume of smoke appeared, the American militia would gather and rush off to confront the raiders. By the time the Americans arrived, British forces had already rowed back to their warships on the bay. It was as frustrating for the militia as it was an effective form of terrorism for the British. The Royal Navy could not win a decisive victory, choosing rather to punish the civilian population along the shores of the Chesapeake.

Instead of teaching the British a lesson, the United States was soon defending itself on several military fronts.

Leading the British forces on the Chesapeake Bay was Admiral Sir George Cockburn. In many respects he was the perfect man to head up this campaign of terror. Cockburn had nothing but disdain for Americans and consequently he was often cruel. At other times he acted with kindness, apparently motivated by a warped sense of chivalry. Cockburn's behavior toward civilians was erratic, but he was a clever and highly capable military commander.

Marylanders could not have dreamed up a worse enemy. The way his name is invoked even today on Maryland's Eastern Shore says something about the man. Although he pronounced his name "Co'burn," Marylanders then and now have disdainfully dubbed him "Cock-burn." As one twenty-first century observer put it, "he was just plain cocky."

1813 was bad enough, but the situation grew worse for Americans in 1814. Napoleon was defeated and exiled to the island of Elba. The tremendous military forces that had been needed to fight Napoleon could now be sent to the United States. President Madison had counted on the British being distracted by the war in Europe. Now there was cause for worry.

The British saw the war as an opportunity to punish the American upstarts. Additionally, to British minds the United States had basically sided with the "French tyrant." Americans had helped the French by draining away resources that could have been used to battle Napoleon. It was time for payback and comeuppance.

British depredations on Chesapeake Bay reached fever pitch. In late August, a British force led in part by Admiral Cockburn sacked and burned the American capital city at Washington. Cocky as ever, Cockburn famously sat down at President Madison's dining table, set for an American victory banquet, and ate with his officers before ordering the White House set ablaze. The United States Capitol also went up in flames. It was a bold victory for the British. But instead of demoralizing Americans the destruction of the capital actually served to galvanize them against the enemy.

Cockburn's stunning capture of the American capital backfired in London. Burning the city was criticized as excessive and barbaric. In the wake of Napoleon's defeat, after decades fighting the French, the British were tired of war. The American war was costly to the depleted British treasury. British leaders knew they could not be lulled into believing that victory in America would be easy.

The Duke of Wellington, who had conquered India and defeated Napoleon, declined to take command of British forces in North America. At this time the Americans had control of the Great Lakes, and Wellington proclaimed that whoever held the lakes held the key to victory.

In addition, the British attack on the city of Baltimore had been a failure despite the Royal Navy's greatly superior military force. That loss was even more pronounced considering British successes during the previous month. Then again, terrorizing waterfront farms and burning a relatively defenseless Washington was child's play compared to the serious business at Baltimore in September 1814. Baltimore was a military and commercial city far more important than Washington and it was well-defended.

Further evidence that the United States would not be easy to conquer came at the battle of New Orleans, where the Redcoats were soundly defeated. After suffering these two major losses, the British embraced the peace treaty that already had been signed.

The intangible outcome of the War of 1812 caused many to see the conflict as unimportant, worthy of little more than a historical footnote. The United States neither lost nor gained territory; there were no great changes in society or in the system of government.

However, Great Britain would never pick another fight with the United States. With the defeat of Tecumseh, effective Indian opposition to westward expansion had ended. The United States would not be a seacoast nation hemmed in by occupied British territory and Indians. It was time to build a vast nation and an American empire.

Quietly, the United States government had withstood war and come out stronger. Flames had destroyed the White House and other government buildings but not the ideals of the young nation. James Madison's Constitution had endured.

No sooner had the war ended, than the rewriting of history began.

The War of 1812 is often given a muddy treatment in high school history textbooks and this may be by design. One theory is that the original histories of the war were written or influenced by New England federalists who had been opposed to the war. New England's Federalist Party members sided with the British and grew rich trading with the enemy even as war raged. At one point, New England bordered on causing civil war by threatening to break away from the United States.

After the war, so the theory goes, the conflict New Englanders had sat out was belittled, its importance watered down. If this theory is even a little true, then what most schoolchildren learn about the War of 1812 is the direct result of nineteenth century spin doctors who downplayed the war and painted Madison as a bumbling president. Consequently,

Americans as a whole know only a little about the War of
1812, most of which was learned in grade school. Students are
told how the national anthem was written and about the
fabulous victory at New Orleans. The history lesson might
even include the legend of Uncle Sam. Supposedly, Samuel
"Uncle Sam" Wilson was an Army food inspector who
stamped *U.S.*—for United States—on barrels of salt meat for
the soldiers. The men joked that the meat was from "Uncle
Sam" and thus an American icon was born. It was not until
World War I that Uncle Sam became truly respectable in
recruiting posters.

Most 1812 historical sites today go unvisited and
unprotected from development. This situation is beginning to
change. The state of Maryland, thanks to the prompting of
Congressman Wayne T. Gilchrest, has finally caught on to
the tourism potential of 1812 and is in the beginning stages of
creating an automobile tour or "trail" that traces the history of
the war.

When compared to America's other wars of the past 225
years, the War of 1812 resulted in a relatively small loss of
life. Estimates are that roughly 2,260 Americans died in actual
combat. Compare that to about 4,000 killed in the
Revolutionary War and 600,000 who died from combat or
disease in the Civil War—a loss of two percent of the nation's
population at that time. In one day of fighting at the battle of
Antietam in September 1862, more than 23,000 Americans
were killed or wounded. Given such terrible loss of life, the
Civil War left wounds that are still healing in America.

"I think that if we look at the history of the United States,
there are two wars that determine what the U.S. looks like
today," said James Madison scholar, Devin Bent. "These are
the War of 1812 and the Civil War. The war with Mexico is a
distant third. If we consider which of the two is more
important, I think it is the War of 1812."

Another legacy of the War of 1812 is that a democracy has never gone to war against another democratic nation. It could be argued that the British are now America's closest ally in a turbulent world. The two nations are united by a common history and a common language. The war was the final catharsis for Anglo-American relations.

Convincing modern Americans that the War of 1812 was important may be an uphill battle. What would be the point? Americans live very much in the present and keep a hopeful eye turned toward the future, yet the lessons of the past have their place. There are those who seek out quiet spots such as Caulk's Field battlefield or old books on the subject. As one re-enactor said, "It's obscure enough to be interesting." By that logic, the hobby of studying 1812 history ranks right up there with collecting salt and pepper shakers or old bottles or maybe even restoring Austin-Healey sports cars.

For some people, there is no doubt that the conflict was important as the Second War of Revolution and a significant victory for Americans. It was something to be proud of, especially for those touched in some way by that long-ago war.

One such person would be Fran Moore, past national president of the Daughters of 1812, which has chapters in forty states. Moore had ancestors in the Revolutionary War, but she takes special pride in those who fought for the United States in 1812. On a hot summer day on Maryland's Eastern Shore, this energetic octogenarian was addressing a group who had come to hear her talk about the War of 1812 on Chesapeake Bay. Her eyes blazed when she got to the topic of British Admiral George Cockburn and his reign of terror.

"Cockburn was a real cocky guy and he thought he could defeat us on the Chesapeake Bay ... but ... he ... did ... not!" she said, stamping her feet for emphasis with each word and setting the blue Daughters of 1812 medal pinned to her blouse swaying. "They came over here and attacked us and they were driven back! We won this war!" That's the very spirit that beat the British and ended their hopes for any hold on America.

2

Re-enacting the War

Living history at St. Leonard's Creek

Hugh Pry looked like a crusty old salt right down to his 1812
sailor's uniform and the gray stubble on his leathery cheeks.
Balanced on his knees was a Charlesville musket, its bright
barrel spotted with rust caused by the morning dew. He
cleaned the musket as we talked, expertly knocking the bands
loose that bound the stock to the barrel. He then began to
shine the metal with a scrap of distinctly twenty-first century,
green scrubby mesh that would have been a more familiar
sight in a modern kitchen than on the nineteenth century
battlefield at St. Leonard's Creek in southern Maryland.

"The War of 1812 was when Americans really started to
think of themselves as a nation," Pry said. Judging by the deft
way he took apart and cleaned the musket, Pry was obviously
very much at home in this recreated version of the nineteenth
century. "We got kicked around a lot but we won the last one
[in New Orleans]."

Pry was one of several War of 1812 re-enactors who had
gathered on a September weekend to re-fight the battle of St.
Leonard's Creek. Also on hand were a few British Redcoats,
who pitched their tents a respectable distance from the
American camp.

Re-enacting a battle is an intense experience. Your musket
barrel gets hot to the touch, your mouth gets dry and gritty

from ripping open paper cartridges filled with black powder and your ears ring for hours after the battle. Your heart thuds wildly as you face a field of the enemy. The guns fire blanks and the bayonets aren't sharp, but a part of your mind doesn't quite believe it. This is about as close to time travel as you can get.

Pry said 1812 re-enactors are not interested in "burning up powder" in big recreated battles. Many have left Civil War re-enacting, tired of the focus on mock warfare. For the most part, 1812 re-enactors take a more thoughtful approach to their military history.

Geoff Graff, a Baltimore resident portraying an 1812-era sailor at the St. Leonard's Creek re-enactment, said he wants to understand what it was like to live during the nineteenth century. He said he feels a connection to that time period and to others like him who are interested in experiencing the past.

"We came here with a real purpose," Graff said of his involvement in re-enacting. "What were their thoughts, how did a bunch of farmers get together and frame a Constitution that still has meaning?"

Graff admitted that his longtime hobby does have drawbacks, including the fact that work on his ninety-year-old home gets neglected. "Let me put it this way," he said. "I've got twenty-three years of deferred maintenance waiting for me at home."

Graff and Pry had come to relive some part of the battle of St. Leonard's Creek, the largest naval battle in Maryland's history, the second half of which took place on June 26, 1814.

The first part of the battle was fought June 8 through 10. Commodore Joshua Barney's flotilla of eighteen vessels had just left Baltimore when he encountered a more powerful British fleet under Admiral Cockburn. The result was a running fight that took place over the course of three days, starting with the battle of Cedar Point at the mouth of the

Patuxent River. With no place else to go, Barney retreated up the Patuxent. Cornered for more than two weeks, he launched the second phase of the battle with a counterattack on the British early on June 26 and managed to break free. The battle was not terribly decisive, but it was a prelude to the British land campaign that would result in the capture and burning of Washington later that summer.

Many of the re-enactors at St. Leonard's Creek were members of the Ship's Company, a group of living historians who portray War of 1812 sailors like those who would have served under Commodore Barney on Chesapeake Bay. The sailors' uniforms were relatively simple. They wore white trousers of a canvas material, blue-and-white checked sailors blouses and waist-length blue wool jackets with brass buttons. Their wide-brimmed hats were made of tarred canvas, often with a long ribbon hanging over the brim. Aboard ship, it was likely many of the sailors in 1812 would have been barefoot, but here on land they wore black leather shoes.

Another of the St. Leonard's Creek re-enactors was Wes Stone, who lived in the nearby town of Lusby. Stone wore a white uniform with black leather crossbelts and brass buckles, high black leather boots, and a black shako—a stovepipe hat about a foot tall with an abbreviated brim similar to that of a horse riding helmet. His musket was propped nearby. Stone explained that he was portraying a soldier in the 36th Infantry.

Stone has been a student of history and a re-enactor long before it was a popular hobby. Back in 1977, he started working for the National Park Service in Alabama, joining several park employees who portrayed Civil War soldiers. Years later, when he moved to southern Maryland, he switched to portraying an 1812 soldier in view of the connection to local history. "Around here in southern Maryland, it's a big story," he said of 1812. "Except for the abolition of slavery, it's really what changed the face of our area."

Like most of the Chesapeake Bay region, southern
Maryland was terrorized by British raiders throughout the
war. While much of the United States was considered to be
frontier or even wilderness in 1812, Maryland had been
settled and farmed for nearly 200 years. Families that had
been working the tidewater farms since the 1600s had become
landed gentry. Many of these old Maryland families moved
on after being burned out repeatedly by the British. They sold
their farms and relocated to areas like Alabama and Kentucky
for a fresh start. War would follow them there half a century
later. Meanwhile, former tenant farmers bought up the land.
"You had this real power shift going on," Stone said.

For Stone, part of the War of 1812's appeal is that it's an
offbeat topic. As an amateur historian he had made a hobby
out of the war. "It wasn't as dramatic as the Revolution and it's
not as gory as the Civil War," he said. Stone described it as
"Part Two" of the Revolution, stating several reasons why
1812 was largely unknown today. These were the same
reasons the conflict wasn't popular among Americans when
the war was being fought. "There was a problem even at the
time in defining the war. It was essentially a war about trade
rights. It just isn't sexy. They had massive trouble at the time
explaining to people what the war was about. It was so ill-
defined."

Despite the lack of "sexiness" attached to 1812, Stone
noted that several historic events occurred that deserve to be
remembered today. For instance, the United States invaded a
foreign country for the first time. There were tremendous
victories like the one at New Orleans and great tragedies like
the destruction of the young nation's capital city.

"How many people ever think about Washington being
burned?" Stone asked. "They burned our capital, for Heaven's
sake."

The general lack of interest in 1812 means the smattering of related living history events in the mid-Atlantic region do not draw large crowds. "1812 re-enacting in general is not as popular as, say, Civil War re-enacting," Stone explained. "The War of 1812 is kind of obscure. As for the re-enactors, it's an older bunch than is usually found on other fields." He compared 1812 re-enacting today to where Civil War re-enacting was in the 1970s, when just about any sort of blue or gray clothing passed for a uniform and a BB gun might double as a musket. The hobby had not caught on with the fervor seen today at events where thousands of re-enactors gather with historically accurate uniforms and weapons. "I just don't think we're going to get that in 1812," he said.

Stone has tried to assemble a unit of fellow 1812 re-enactors centered around Jefferson Patterson Park and Museum located at the battlefield, but the costs involved have been prohibitive. The $1,500 expense to outfit each soldier in the basic uniform and musket, not including camping gear or other accouterments, is a determent. "A guy who is only going to go out twice a year has to think hard about spending that kind of money," Stone said.

It is true that re-enacting is not an inexpensive hobby. Re-enactors ultimately rely on authenticity to create the sort of time travel experience that helps them understand the life of an 1812 soldier. While enthusiasm for the past can be had for free, the trappings that bring it to life come with a hefty price tag.

As someone who has dabbled in Civil War re-enacting, I am embarrassed to tell people outside the world of living history enthusiasts that I have spent $95 for a pair of peg-soled leather brogans with heel plates that ring like horseshoes while crossing pavement, or $75 for a logwood-dyed kepi that will fade nicely in the summer sun, or $195 for a hand-sewn jean-wool shell jacket in Confederate butternut that's going to get covered with gunpowder stains and mud. Maybe only fellow re-enactors can understand this sort of madness.

If you want to get started in 1812 re-enacting, keep your credit card handy. For example, a company that makes and sells period uniforms and equipment lists the following items on its website:

- Brown Bess carbine $425
- British Bearskin (worn by grenadiers) $595
- Sword bayonet and scabbard $95
- 1796 Heavy Cavalry Sword $195
- Baker Rifle $450
- Stovepipe Shako $225
- Stovepipe Shako Plate $55
- Gorget, British 1812 Pattern $95

Remember that word "authenticity"? Clothing and other items for re-enactors aren't like the mass-produced items found at the local shopping mall. Neither are they like those gray or blue felt hats with cardboard brims sold at souvenir shops in Gettysburg or the tri-corner felt ones sold in Williamsburg. Consider, for example, the $225 shako that would have been worn by British troops in America. These replica hats feature wool felt from Poland, linen from Ireland, wool yarn from Iceland, leather from traditional tanneries in England, and lace from England and France. That is authenticity. It does not come cheap.

Re-enactors have a passion for certain replica equipment much as the soldiers of 1812 must have had, especially when it comes to their muskets. Weapons of the day relied on using flints—literally slivers of rock—to strike a metal plate, creating sparks that ignite the pinch of gunpowder in a "pan" at the base of the plate. That small explosion is channeled into the musket barrel, where it sets off the main charge of gunpowder. Firing a musket thus requires a chain reaction that takes place in a split second: trigger pull trips hammer, flint hits metal and sparks, sparks light powder in the pan, that small blast sets off the charge in the barrel, which propels the musket ball. It's easy for a malfunction in that chain reaction to occur. Hence the expression "flash in the pan" for something that starts out strong and then fizzles, a common failing of muskets where the powder in the pan sparks but fails to set off the main charge. In the nineteenth century, a flash in the pan was not a good thing on the battlefield or when hunting for dinner.

Spectators at 1812 events will notice many "flash in the pan" episodes. Seeing so many misfires, it surprised me that anyone was actually shot with a flintlock musket during the War of 1812. When I asked Doug Wicklund at the National Firearms Museum about that, he informed me that keeping a musket in top working condition takes constant attention that re-enactors sometimes don't give. No one's life is hanging in the balance as it did in 1812.

When the charge of gunpowder in the barrel exploded, it sent forth a hurtling ball of lead. The inside of a musket barrel is smooth, without the modern spiral grooves known as rifling. Musket balls do not fit the barrel snugly and rattle around on the way out. That smooth bore makes a bullet inaccurate and short-ranged. Picture the difference like this: get a bad grip on a football and it wobbles and flips end over end when you throw a pass; rifling gives a bullet a nice spin in the same way your fingers roll off a football to make a long, straight "bullet-like" pass.

In addition to muskets, there were a few rifles in use during 1812, notably the famous Kentucky Long Rifle in America and the British Baker Rifle, made well-known in Bernard Cornwell's *Sharpe's Rifles* novels set during the

Napoleonic era. Rifles of the day could shoot accurately at long range, but they were slow to load and unreliable in the field. Black powder fouled the rifling, prompting some British riflemen to urinate down their barrels to clean out the gunpowder.

For re-enactors, heat exhaustion is probably the biggest danger. The muskets used in mock battles also have the potential to cause harm. Safety always comes first. Re-enactors are warned to aim above a person's head. They never fire when too close to another re-enactor. Powder is poured down musket muzzles but ramrods are never used to tamp the load. A ramrod left in a musket barrel during the heat of battle can become a dangerous projectile.

The weapon carried by most British troops and sometimes used by Americans in 1812, was the Brown Bess musket, that workhorse of the British military. Much as the M-16 might be viewed today by the United States armed forces, the Brown Bess has a sturdy look about it. These muskets have a dark brown finish with a "gooseneck" type hammer that holds the flint.

Though the Brown Bess may have been primitive and short-ranged, it fired a .75 caliber lead ball, roughly the same size as the "pumpkin ball" slugs used by deer hunters in modern 12-gauge shotguns. Imagine a row of orderly British troops advancing to within fifty yards with 12-gauge shotguns spitting lead pumpkin balls and you can begin to understand why untrained American militia melted away during battles.

Another musket favored by Americans at the time was the Charlesville (pronounced Shar-lay-ville), named after the armory in the French town where they were made. An American copy of the Charlesville was made at the federal armory at Harpers Ferry, Virginia (later to become West Virginia), and used right up through the Mexican War. The Charlesville was built along more graceful lines than the

Brown Bess, with three bands holding the barrel to the stock. Remember earlier how re-enactor Hugh Pry expertly knocked the bands of his Charlesville loose to clean the barrel? The Charlesville musket looks much like the Enfield favored by Confederate troops during the Civil War. Charlesvilles were .69 caliber weapons, meaning their bore was similar to today's 20-gauge shotguns.

During 1812, most American troops in the Chesapeake region were militia who reported for duty carrying whatever weapon happened to be suspended from pegs above the fireplace. For many citizen-soldiers, that firearm was not a military weapon but a well-used household fowling piece employed to bag ducks, geese, rabbits and squirrels for the dinner table. These weapons fired handfuls of lead shot and could hardly be considered combat weapons sufficient to take on the troops that had conquered Napoleon.

Fowling pieces were not designed to be fitted with bayonets. In an era when tactics favored an attacker that rushed a position and finished the job with bayonets, American militia was left at a disadvantage. It is clear from looking at the replica weapons and equipment of re-enactors that British troops in 1812 had a distinct edge.

Weapons aside, why would anyone want to be a British re-enactor? What sort of red-blooded American would want to don a red coat?

"I think it's got that same cachet as with British Revolutionary War re-enactors," said Wes Stone. "It's hard core."

According to Stone, most British re-enactors in the mid-Atlantic are Royal Marines, the troops featured in C.S. Forester's Horatio Hornblower novels. He said it is likely that the Hornblower books and recent film series have been an influence on American re-enactors becoming British Marines.

"They're not too bright," he said, describing marines of the

day. "They behave well. They do their drill. They do their
duty. There's a sense of admiration for their professionalism."

One of the Redcoats on hand for the St. Leonard's Creek
re-enactment was an actual Englishman. Until about ten years
ago, Terry Crabb was a resident of Essex in Southeastern
England. He now lives in Richmond, Virginia. Crabb got
started in re-enacting a few years ago when he attended a
Revolutionary War event and noticed many blue-coated
American re-enactors but few British Redcoats. "I decided I
had to increase their number by one," he said with a mild
British accent.

Tall and gray-haired, Crabb looked rather regal in his
uniform. His stovepipe shako with the brass plate stamped
with "44"—his regiment's number –made him appear even
taller. He wore a red coat with yellow facings around the
buttons and collar, and white pants. He had been an 1812 re-
enactor for about one year.

When asked why he chose to re-enact, Crabb replied,
"There are as many reasons as there are people." He added
that he likes the hobby because it gets him outdoors after a
week in the office and takes him to new places. "You have that
balance, all the cares of the week fade away. It's a good family
hobby, too."

Crabb pointed out that choosing to become a British re-
enactor can be more than a matter of birth. He said 1812 and
Revolutionary War re-enactors put on red coats because they
have something in common with British soldiers of that era.
"The people portraying the British are those people who are
for law and order," he said. "If they were transported back to
that time, they would not be for the Revolution."

A reproduction of an 1812 recruitment handbill distributed
by members of the 1st Company, 2nd Battalion Royal Marines
re-enactment group in the Baltimore area reflects the appeal
marines had for British men of the era:

The Single Young Man on his Return to Port, finds himself enabled to cut a Draft on Shore with his GIRL and his GLASS, that might be envied by a Nobleman.

For a young man who might not know where his next meal was coming from, the handbill offers these further enticements for joining the Royal Marines:

The Daily Allowance of a Marine when embarked, is – One Pound of BEEF or PORK, – One Pound of BREAD, – Flour, Raisins, Butter, Cheese, Oatmeal, Molasses, Tea, Sugar, &c.&c And a Pint of the best WINE or Half a Pint of the best RUM or BRANDY; together with a Pint of LEMONADE. They have likewise in warm Countries, a plentiful allowance of the choicest FRUIT. And what can be more handsome than the Royal Marine Proportion of PRIZE MONEY, when a Serjeant shares equal with the First Class of Petty Officers . . .

This sense of being paid to get the job done, of doing the dirty work for a paycheck, does create a certain feeling of pride. Marines were professionals. What young British lad wouldn't want to be a marine, putting American farmers armed with fowling pieces on the run? That spirit remains among British re-enactors.

Another difference between 1812 re-enacting compared to the Civil War scene is that there is no undercurrent of politics among participants. The political issues of 1812 do not inspire passionate feelings in the twenty-first century and most Americans today cannot get themselves worked up about the burning of Washington or other British outrages from 187 years ago. By contrast, talk around the campfires at Civil War events sometimes resonates with painful, unsettled issues that continue to divide Americans.

That evening, the 1812 re-enactors took part in "Tavern Night" in a barn at the park. Members of the community poured in to enjoy the live period music. Some people played checkers and backgammon by candlelight at picnic tables under the stars. On the wall of the barn behind the stage two flags were hanging side by side. One was the American flag with fifteen stars and fifteen stripes that flew during the War of 1812, the other was the Union Jack.

With the candlelight and music, it was easy to leave the twenty-first century behind and travel back in time to another era. The re-enactors circulated through the crowd or sat together at a long table with mugs of Sam Adams and Chesapeake Gold beer, red uniforms mixed with blue. Looking at the smiling faces and the flags on the wall, the bloodshed of 1812 seemed like a terrible and tragic mistake between old friends.

3

War on the High Seas
Aboard the Pride of Baltimore II

It was a sunny, late October day and the *Pride of Baltimore II* rode gently on the sharp tug of current in the Chesapeake and Delaware Canal. Swells from passing barges and pleasure boats barely moved the ship moored in front of the popular waterfront Schaefer's Canal House restaurant in Chesapeake City. A tantalizing smell of crab cakes wafted from the restaurant kitchen.

As so often happens with the War of 1812 in Maryland, history had literally turned up in my backyard in the form of the *Pride of Baltimore II*, a tall ship built as a replica of a wartime privateer. From my back porch windows I could see *Pride II* docked on the other side of the Chesapeake Canal.

Given such surroundings, a visit aboard the *Pride II* was marked with an air of nautical ceremony, complete with a crew member to welcome aboard guests at the gangplank. However, this ship's history turns out to be anything but polite. The pedigree of the *Pride II* is gritty and glorious.

The *Pride II* is owned by the state of Maryland. It bears the distinction of being "II" because the first replica tall ship sank in a storm in 1986 with a tragic loss of life. The *Pride II* visits ports across the United States and around the world as a goodwill ambassador from the people of Maryland.

In 1812, the ship would not have been so welcome, at least

not in any English ports.

"Careful, he may be a spy for the British," growled a barefoot sailor in striped shirt and canvas trousers when I came aboard with my notebook.

It's a good thing that Michael Buck was only kidding, considering he presided over a formidable armory of cutlasses and flintlock pistols spread out on the deck. Buck portrayed an able-bodied seaman who would have helped man this ship in the nineteenth century. He made his twenty-first century home in the town of Boring, and his shipmate, Jeff Miller, jokingly pointed out that the town was located "between two haystacks" in Baltimore County.

Miller lived in Havre de Grace, a nearby waterfront town that received a drubbing at the hands of the British, which might explain why the two sailors were suspicious. Miller also portrayed an able-bodied seaman, decked out for shore duty in white trousers, blue wool coat and a cross belt bearing a large, shiny brass buckle. He wore a top hat made of tarred material. Bearded, bespectacled and wearing wool gloves with the fingertips cut out, Miller looked something like a militant version of Fagan from *Oliver Twist.*

The two opted against throwing me overboard as a British spy despite all the questions I asked. Instead, they educated me about the colorful career of the Baltimore clipper ship on which *Pride II* is modeled.

That ship was the *Chasseur*, which Miller was helpful enough to spell. "It's Frenchie for 'Hunter' or 'Chaser'," he explained. The only clue to the vessel's heritage is a ship's boat on deck, which bears the name *Chasseur* on its stern.

The *Chasseur* was part of a famous class of sailing vessels known as Baltimore clipper ships. These topsail schooners had two distinct, raked masks and the graceful design of a racing yacht. Even someone who doesn't know a thing about boats can see that *Pride II* has beautiful lines, with raked masts that give even a casual observer the impression that this ship was built for speed. The *Pride II* lists its maximum sailing speed as fourteen knots.

Baltimore was famed for its fast clipper ships, many of which were built in the Fells Point neighborhood, better known today for bars than boats. Back in 1812, the port city was the base for a whole fleet of American privateer vessels.

Early in the War of 1812, America's success on the high seas was a bright counterpoint to its dismal showing on land. Even so, the numbers did not favor the United States. The American navy had seven ships, only six of which would fight in the war. The Royal Navy had 191 "ships of the line" intended, as the name implies, to fight in a line of battle on the sea. Each ship had sixty to eighty guns. The British fleet also had 245 frigates armed with thirty to fifty guns apiece.

Not all these Royal Navy ships were used against the United States during the War of 1812. The British had interests worldwide to defend. Navy ships also blockaded the coast of Africa in an attempt to halt the slave trade. Years of war with France had left many British ships undermanned with inexperienced crews. Nevertheless, with Napoleon's defeat, the American war received far more attention from the mighty Royal Navy as vessels were freed up to fight the United States.

The ships of the small American navy were well-designed and had an almost magical ability to capture the wind. They also were captained and crewed by veterans of the Barbary Wars. Unlike the American army, the navy had skills honed in combat.

As the war began, there were several American victories at sea. The *USS President* sank the British sloop *Little Belt* and then crippled the frigate *Belvidera*. The *USS Constitution* under Havre de Grace resident Commodore John Rodgers sank the frigate *HMS Guerriere*. The *USS Wasp* captured the brig *HMS Frolic*. The *USS United States* captured the *HMS Macedonian*. Under the new captain William Bainbridge, the *Constitution* sank the *HMS Java*. The list went on and on, causing genuine alarm for the British government. The thought that the upstart Americans and their tiny navy could win so many victories over the Royal Navy was disturbing to a nation that considered its fleet invincible. The sheer number of British ships and an effective blockade of United States ports would soon overwhelm the Americans, but the early months of war on the high seas were glorious for the United States.

Another famous American navy 1812 ship was the *USS Constellation*, currently docked at Baltimore's Inner Harbor. It is generally accepted that this ship is not the same vessel built in 1797 that saw service during the War of 1812. The *Constellation* evidently underwent a massive rebuild in 1853 that basically transformed it into an altogether different vessel. Debate continues over whether or not bits and pieces of the original vessel were recycled, thus giving the *Constellation* a material connection to 1812.

Not all the victories at sea came from official navy vessels. America also relied heavily on its privateer fleet to harass the enemy's shipping and the attacks began to have a telling effect on British trade.

Privateers were a sort of government-sanctioned pirate fleet that operated under a Letter of Marque and Reprisal issued by the president. To a lesser extent, the British also made use of privateers. British or American, the role of a privateer ship was to prey upon the enemy's merchant fleet. The privateer took possession any captured ships and cargo, which meant huge profits for the privateer's crew and owners.

In the twenty-first century, privateers have gone the way of cutlasses and black powder. Most nations abolished the practice in the Declaration of Paris in 1856. Along with Spain,

Mexico and Venezuela, the United States did not sign the treaty but decided to keep its wartime options open. The U.S. never again resorted to privateering, although the Confederate States of America made use of privateers in the 1860s.

By the end of the War of 1812, there were 500 registered American privateers. Only a few of these ships did any real damage to the enemy's merchant shipping. American privateers cost the British hundreds of lives and millions of dollars in lost ships and cargo. Estimates are that as many as 1,700 prizes were taken, most within the last year and a half of war. That works out to about two ships lost per day, a devastating loss to British merchants.

Operating a privateer was a business enterprise. Many, like *Chasseur*, began life as merchant vessels but were turned to privateering out of sheer financial necessity on the part of their owners. "There just isn't any merchant trade during a blockade," Miller said. Groups of wealthy businessmen formed partnerships to outfit idle merchant ships as privateers. Guns and powder, cutlasses and grappling hooks were purchased, stores of food were laid in, and the salaries of crews were paid. There were huge risks. The entire ship could be lost. However, a lucky ship could make its owners, captain and crew rich. Due to the British blockade on the United States, cargoes of coffee, rum, fruit and silk seized by privateers brought high prices.

"When there's a shortage, people with money will pay a premium," Miller said, delivering his explanations in a hearty, salty dog style true to a sailor of the era. "The ladies in Philadelphia and Baltimore were still looking for something to wear to their parties."

Miller took umbrage to any comparison between privateers and pirates. When asked the difference between the two, he drew himself up and sniffed, "Pirates are lawless." A ship's crew captured by pirates could expect wholesale slaughter.

Privateers operated under rather gentlemanly rules. They were expected to treat captured crews with respect. In turn, captive captains and crew members of privateers were considered prisoners of war, not criminals. Captured pirates, on the other hand, usually came to a quick end involving a length of rope and a yardarm.

Privateers were not interested in fighting naval battles with British ships of the line. Most privateers did not have the firepower to compete with Royal Navy vessels, which could throw far more iron—cannonballs—than any privateer trading broadsides with them. Their goal was to capture merchant ships and make money. They relied on speed to overtake merchant vessels rather than firepower.

Anyone who has read a Patrick O'Brian novel or seen the recent Horatio Hornblower films knows the basic drill involved in capturing a merchant vessel. The privateer crew comes alongside the hapless merchantman, tosses grappling hooks into the rigging so the two ships are locked together, then swarms aboard. More than anything else, a privateer relied on sheer numbers to overwhelm the merchant ship's crew. There would be a short, swift fight, a prize crew would be put aboard to sail the ship to a harbor where it could be sold for a handsome profit, and the privateer would sail off in search of its next victim.

Normally, Miller said, a ship such as *Chasseur* was crewed by a dozen men, but as many as one hundred might be crammed aboard the 109-foot vessel for a privateer cruise. The more men the better; the length and success of a privateer cruise was limited only by the number of prize crews it could put aboard captured vessels.

The *Chasseur* was one of the most legendary of Baltimore's privateer ships. *Chasseur* had such a successful career as a privateer that when the ship returned to the city on March 25, 1815, from a voyage that would make the history books, a local newspaper called *The Niles Weekly Register* dubbed the ship, crew and captain "the Pride of Baltimore." The name stuck.

"It's just like how Lou Gehrig got his nickname as 'The Pride of the Yankees,' " Miller said. "He didn't sign his name that way—it just caught on."

The British controlled the Chesapeake Bay, ravaging Maryland's waterfront towns at will. American privateers owned the high seas. Miller explained that *Chasseur* and another ship, *Comet*, owned by Baltimore captain Thomas Boyle, made the equivalent in today's dollars of hundreds of millions in profits. The *Comet* had the distinction of earning the greatest profit of any other privateer ship during that war. The *Comet* and *Chasseur* operated off the coasts of England and Ireland under the very nose of the mighty Royal Navy, capturing ships loaded with luxury goods.

Boyle was a particularly bold captain. During the summer of 1814, while his ship prowled off the British Isles, he sent a "Proclamation of Blockage" to be posted on the door of Lloyd's of London, the shipping underwriter. The idea that one ship might declare a blockade was nothing short of outrageous. Captain Boyle lived up to his boast. Historians credit *Chasseur* with capturing more than thirty prizes during the war.

There was at least one episode in *Chasseur's* career when a case of mistaken identity brought the ship into a confrontation with a Royal Navy ship. On February 26, 1814, crew members sighted what they thought was a merchant vessel off the coast of Cuba. The *Chasseur* overtook the ship, discovering that it was the Royal Navy schooner *St. Lawrence*. It was too late to take flight, so the two ships fought a ten-minute battle before the *St. Lawrence* surrendered.

Captain Boyle wrote *Chasseur's* owners,

> I should not willingly, perhaps, have sought a contest
> with a King's vessel, knowing it is not our object. But
> my expectations at first were a valuable vessel, and a
> valuable cargo. When I found myself deceived, the
> honor of the flag intrusted to my care was not to be
> disgraced by flight.

Ironically, the very characteristics that made Baltimore
clippers like *Chasseur* such good privateers rendered them
commercial albatrosses after the war. The clippers were fast
and light, but could not carry much cargo. Their owners were
left with three choices to keep their investment profitable.
Baltimore clippers specialized in carrying expensive goods
speedily from China, became mercenaries for South
American nations in rebellion with Spain, or entered the
illegal but lucrative slave trade. The third option helped make
Baltimore one of the leading slave-trading cities up until the
Civil War. As for *Chasseur*, the ship finished out her career in
the service of the Spanish navy in the Caribbean.

It is the *Pride's* 1812 heyday that Marylanders celebrate.
When *Pride II* visits Maryland waterfront towns, Miller and
Buck often go with the ship to places like Chesapeake City,
St. Michaels and Solomon's Island. Also along is Miller's wife,
Kelly, who dresses in clothes of the era and describes a
woman's role and domestic life. The three are members of the
Fort McHenry Guard, an 1812 re-enactors group. On these
trips, the Millers and Buck share the ship's history and answer
questions about seafaring life in the early 1800s. When asked
if Marylanders know much about the War of 1812, the two
men looked at each other and there was a long silence. "That's
a sore point," Buck finally said. "Marylanders don't know
their history."

Miller said that some visitors aboard *Pride II* know the highlights, such as a vague knowledge of the Star-Spangled Banner or Fort McHenry. "Beyond that, not many people understand what happened," he said. "The British basically turned the entire Chesapeake into an English lake."

Miller and Buck recounted some of the 1812 devastation that took place in the upper Chesapeake Bay: the burning of Havre de Grace, Fredericktown and Georgetown, Frenchtown, Caulk's Field. They also mentioned some of the heroes of the war.

"Joshua Barney should be a childhood hero to all the children in Maryland," Miller said. "He was something of a duffer in age when the war came along, but he was an incredible leader. It was him and his flotilla who held the rearguard during the battle of Bladensburg."

Miller acknowledged that the results of the War of 1812 were mostly elusive. "When the war was over we hadn't gained or lost anything," he said. "We ended up exactly where we started."

After a pleasant afternoon aboard the old privateer, I said goodbye to these sailors, who once again loudly raised their suspicions that I might be a British spy. I left with some reluctance, only because their good-natured interest in history felt contagious.

The next morning, *Pride II* was still anchored on the far side of the canal. School children came aboard during the day, and crew members hoisted the sails for them. A photographer from the local newspaper came down and took pictures, which were published in the next day's edition. The photo caption read: "The ship is a replica of the famed War of 1812 topsail schooners known as 'Baltimore Clippers.' The fast ships often were used as privateer vessels to raid British shipping."

The *Pride II* spent one more night and then motored away.

I was drinking my morning coffee on the sun porch as the ship turned into the channel, its sails not yet up but its flag and banners streaming from the masts. It was just as *Chasseur* must have appeared in 1814 as it left Baltimore harbor for its famous cruise, looking not so much like a ship as a bird of prey, ready for a hunt that would go down in history.

4

Flames on Chesapeake Bay

*Old Bohemia, the Legend of Kitty Knight
and the burning of Georgetown*

The article in the *Cecil Whig* promised a "Rite for Visiting a Cemetery" following Mass at St. Francis Xavier Shrine on Memorial Day. It noted that the cemetery was the final resting place of veterans from the War of 1812, the Civil War and "various wars of the twentieth century." The article added, "Among the celebrities interred there is Kitty Knight, local heroine during the British bombardment of Georgetown, Md., during the War of 1812."

Curious about the final resting place of Kitty Knight and what a "Rite for Visiting a Cemetery" might be, I rose early that Monday and headed for the church, which is known locally as "Old Bohemia." The site is nearly as remote now as when Catholics founded a church there in 1704. All around the brick church the spring fields were lush and green under an overcast sky. The only sound was the singing from the church.

Inside, Father Thomas Flowers was celebrating Mass. Slowly, he led the congregation through the ritualistic Catholic service, then paused to deliver his homily. As befit the holiday, he talked about war, especially the fact that popular entertainment often glorifies what is a grisly and heartbreaking business.

"Like Christ, they were asked to bear a cross they could never fully understand," Flowers told the congregation. "When I was a kid I used to watch those war movies with all those guns and cannons and it was great entertainment . . . but how painful it must be for the loved ones who lost someone. Those scars never go away."

An American flag stood prominently near the altar. Most of the congregation looked old enough to be World War II veterans, gray-haired and fragile. They knelt on the bare wood floor, even though it must have been painful on their old knees. Mine already ached.

Flowers wrapped up his homily. "We ask the Lord not only to not take our liberty for granted, but to use it wisely."

The song during communion was *The Battle Hymn of the Republic*, a stirring and deeply religious song sung by Union soldiers during the Civil War. As the Mass ended, the congregation filed out to the cemetery while singing, *My Country 'Tis of Thee*, which was included in the hymn book. Oddly enough, the national anthem was not among the more than 150 songs listed in the book.

The cemetery rite consisted of a few prayers from the priest and a group recitation of *Hail Mary*. The congregation then sang *Faith of Our Fathers*.

As the crowd drifted apart after the final blessing, I went in search of Kitty Knight. Her large marble vault was almost directly against the eastern wall of the church. Nothing on the vault identifies her as the heroine of the Battle of Georgetown, although a small flag was planted nearby. A couple of the congregation's elderly men had also sought her out. "I was upset when that restaurant closed," one man said, referring to the Kitty Knight house, a restaurant that occupies the heroine's old home. "Glad to see it's back in business."

Her inscription reads:

Miss Catharine Knight
d. Nov. 22, 1855
Age 79

Flags marked several of the graves, but none belonged to War of 1812 veterans. Kitty Knight seemed to be the only resident with an 1812 connection. I did come across the headstone of Henry Van Bibber Crawford, Co. B, 1st Md. Cavalry, Confederate. He died on January 14, 1897 at age sixty-three. "Death was sudden," according to the headstone. A small United States flag was stuck beside his grave, and I had to wonder what this old Rebel would have thought about that.

The early priests of Old Bohemia were buried in a weedy, walled plot behind the church. A small bronze plaque identified the priests, including Thomas Poulton, S.J., founder of the church academy where at least two signers of the Declaration of Independence received their early education. The plaque listed Father Poulton as having been born in England in 1697 and dying on January 23, 1749. Other early priests buried there were Thomas Hodgson, born in 1682 in England, and Joseph Creaton, also born in England in 1679. Creaton became founder of Old St. Joseph's Church in Philadelphia. I felt a slight sense of awe standing beside the graves of men born more than three hundred years before.

Sister Stephanie Wilson of the Ursuline Convent in Wilmington, Delaware, sidled up next to me as I scribbled information from the plaque into my notebook. At first I didn't realize this gray-haired woman was a nun, although the large wooden cross she wore around her neck should have been a clue. Her wealth of knowledge about local church history was what finally gave her away.

We talked about what the church must have been like in colonial days. She had a practical view of the early Catholics at this spot, who evidently welcomed many immigrants to the area. "They needed people to work," she said with a hand sweeping across the empty countryside that was once a Jesuit plantation.

Our talk turned to 1812. Back then, America was giving people opportunities they had never dreamed of in Europe. No matter how well their frigates controlled the nearby Chesapeake Bay, this was a new country that must have galled the British leaders and their strict class system. America was truly the land of opportunity in the early 1800s.

Kitty Knight defended her corner of America that day in Georgetown harbor when the old world encroached upon it. She stood up to King George, saved her home, and brought a measure of celebrity to a lonely country cemetery.

Georgetown and its twin village, Fredericktown, are located on opposite banks of the Sassafras River. Ironically, considering the destruction that Royal Marines would bring there, the villages were named after the sons of King George II. It is one of the earliest areas explored and settled by the British in America. Captain John Smith met the local Indians there in 1608, giving the river the Indian name Tockwough. British settlers renamed the river for the abundance of sassafras trees, whose roots were valued for medicinal purposes.

The beginnings of a village had sprung up by 1707 and at least one area plantation dates to 1681. By the time the British arrived to burn the villages, they had been established for more than a century. As a port that connected to overland routes to Philadelphia and New York, famous travelers such as George Washington, Thomas Jefferson and James Madison had all passed through Georgetown. This was not some entirely forgotten rural outpost, but the villages had little strategic or military value.

None of that mattered to Admiral Cockburn, whose

marines sailed up the Sassafras River on May 5, 1813. The British left their larger warships behind in the open waters of the bay. Accounts say the British had 500 men in five thirty-foot barges, each with small cannons.

On land, from the hillside near Kitty Knight's house and looking out over the river, a little imagination helps you travel back in time. Watching the British flotilla approach must have felt unreal as the enemy fleet descended upon the peaceful village.

Cockburn, trying as usual to appear magnanimous, sent two captured slaves to warn the Americans not to resist. If no shots were fired, he would only burn the ships at anchor and the storehouses.

His request would not be met, as even Cockburn must have known. The Americans were not about to give up without a fight. American militia had built a makeshift fort overlooking the river. About 400 men and some cannon were under the command of Colonel T.W. Veasey, who lived on a nearby farm. If for no other reason than to save face, he ordered his men to open fire. The Americans put up a hot resistance for about half an hour until the British threatened to overwhelm the fort. The militia melted back into the countryside, some men returning to the villages to save what they could before the British arrived.

Dr. Edward Scott, a witness to the attack described the scene in a letter the next day:

> I saw the smoke and flame rise in quick succession from the burning villages and as soon as the enemy departed, visited their ruins. Without one or two exceptions the houses saved are most materially injured—their doors, windows, mantle pieces and staircases being burned and hacked with hatchets. Some of the inhabitants had removed their furniture, others had not been so

provident and suffered most severely. No property, however trifling, valuable or sacred escaped the reparious hands of the foe. Women and children and even Blacks were plundered nearly of their all. Beds were cut open and the feathers scattered abroad. Desks, looking glasses, cupboards, tables, chairs, clocks, etc. were shivered to fragments. Even Bibles were taken off for the avowed purpose of making cartridge. With the honourable exception of a Capt. Myres and one or two others, Admiral Cockburn's officers behaved in the same inhuman, indecent style, saluting respectable citizens and even delicate females with the most vulgar guardism.

The British burned mechanic shops, granaries, store houses, twenty-three private homes in the villages, several area farmhouses, taverns, a large schooner at anchor and three smaller ships. Smoke and flames filled the May sky.

Into the midst of this scene of destruction strode the proud and beautiful Kitty Knight. After months at sea, what British officer could resist her charms? You can almost imagine a scene in a movie set to a stirring soundtrack as the brave heroine faces down the handsome Admiral Cockburn in his regal blue uniform with smoke and flames swirling about them.

Local legends have grown over the years that describe Kitty Knight waving the stars and stripes in the faces of the British or chasing off British marines with a broom. Her personal account, written many years after the attack, is more matter-of-fact.

The British, after landing, commenced to burn all the lower part of the town, which was largely of frame. There were, however, two brick buildings on top of the hill—they are there today—which had not as yet been fired. In one of them was an old lady sick and almost destitute, and to this building the Admiral and his sailors and marines proceeded at a rapid gait. I followed them but before I got to the top of the hill, they had set fire to the house in which the old lady lay. I immediately called the attention of the Admiral to the fact that they were about to burn up a human being and that a woman, and I pleaded with him to make his men put the fire out. This I finally succeeded in doing, when they immediately went next door, not forty feet distant and fired the second of the brick houses. I told the commanding officer that as the wind was blowing toward the other house the old lady would be burned up anyhow, when, apparently affected by my appeal, he called his men off but left the fire burning, saying 'Come on, boys!' As they went out of the door, one of them struck his boarding-axe through a panel of the door.

When the British finally rowed away, the destruction of the town was complete. Some accounts say the British left the smoking ruins of as many as 300 buildings. This number is almost certainly exaggerated, but there is no doubt that the devastation of the twin towns was substantial. Families whose homes and storehouses burned were left destitute. Given the scene of destruction in 1813, it is no wonder people on the Eastern Shore still speak spitefully of Admiral Cockburn.

Father Flowers at Old Bohemia Church compared Kitty Knight to Barbara Frietchie, the brave woman whom James Greenleaf Whittier immortalized in his famous poem about patriotism. The beginning of the poem might be familiar to those who once had to memorize poetry in school.

Up from the meadows rich with corn
Clear in the cool September morn ...

Frietchie waved her Union flag defiantly at Confederate
troops marching through Frederick and drew musket fire for
her patriotism. From her attic window overlooking the street,
she shouted at the Rebels.

"Shoot, if you must, this old gray head,
But spare your country's flag," she said.

Whittier's stirring poem is not based entirely on truth. It is
unlikely Barbara Frietchie was actually the woman waving
the flag. Like so much patriotic poetry it is a tale based on
allegory. As far as I know, no one has written a poem about
Kitty Knight. She does star in a 1935 novel by Gertrude
Crownfield entitled, *Capturing Kitty: A romance of the
Sassafras River.* The dwelling she defended from the British is
now the restaurant and inn known as The Kitty Knight
House.

There may have been a dark side to Kitty Knight. In his
book *Lost Towns of the Eastern Shore*, author Donald
Shomette relates how the same anger that drove Kitty Knight
to challenge the British was unleashed on defenseless victims
as well.

Kitty was a wealthy young woman known for her beauty.
As a pretty young belle she attended balls in Philadelphia,
where she captured the eye of General Washington, among
others. It seems she was madly in love with a rich young man
from the area named Perry Spencer and they were to be
married. One day Spencer came upon a scene involving his
fiancé that disturbed him greatly. Unseen, he watched as Kitty
Knight fell into a rage and severely beat a slave boy whom she
thought had mistreated her horse. Appalled, the young man

wrote her a note ending their engagement and never saw her again.

What became of Kitty Knight? Her brave defiance of Cockburn made her a heroine at a time when Americans needed one badly. She never married and lived out her life in Georgetown in the very house she had saved, dying at age seventy-nine in 1855.

The attack on Georgetown and Fredericktown came at the end of a campaign of terror on the upper bay. On April 29, 1813, the British attacked and burned a key Chesapeake Bay port at Frenchtown.

Located on the Elk River, Frenchtown was where vessels deposited their cargo or took on a new one. There was no water route beyond that point, so the cargo would then be carried across the narrow Delmarva Peninsula by wagon, either all the way to Philadelphia or to a ship waiting at the port town of New Castle on the Delaware Bay. It was a cumbersome system, to be sure. In 1829, the Chesapeake and Delaware Canal opened to provide a water route between the Chesapeake and Delaware bays. The opening of the canal meant ships no longer had to stop at Frenchtown to off-load cargo. This spelled the true end of the village more so than the British attack. Frenchtown never really recovered from being put to the torch and today almost nothing remains at this spot on the Elk River to indicate that it was once an important shipping center.

In October 1999, a team of graduate students from East Carolina University and underwater archaeologists from the Maryland Historical Trust descended on Frenchtown to search for clues to the British attack. Using the latest sonar devices, they searched the murky Elk River. The water is about eight feet deep and has a color and consistency similar to chocolate milk. Any attempt at underwater exploration using divers was difficult. Sonar images revealed the wreckage of a sixty-foot ship buried in the mud. Divers did manage to collect bits and pieces of the wreck, which confirmed that it was an 1800s-era vessel. The researchers may very well have found one of the ships burned by the British in 1813.

After Frenchtown, the British moved on to sack and burn Elkton, a busy crossroads town at the head of the Chesapeake Bay. It was not the first time the British had set their sights on the town. In 1777, during the Revolutionary War, Lord Howe landed 15,000 British and Hessian troops near Elkton and occupied the town. George Washington and the Marquis de Lafayette came within a whisker of being captured when they went to spy on the British. Nearly inside the British lines, they were trapped by darkness and a summer storm.

Thirty-six years later the British expected another easy invasion, considering their recent success at Georgetown and Frenchtown. But at Elkton, the British were about to get an unpleasant surprise.

5

These Times Have Been Troublesome
Frenchtown, Fort Defiance and the Defense of Elkton

When the local militia saw the smoke rising to the south of Elkton, they rushed to get ready for the British. The defenders knew the British would come up the Elk River that led toward town, so two small batteries of guns were placed along the shore and named Fort Defiance and Fort Hollingsworth. An iron chain was stretched across the river to prevent British ships from having an easy passage. Ignoring these defensive measures, Royal Marines stubbornly rowed up the river in several gunboats.

The river narrowed and became Little Elk Creek—a waterway deep enough for a schooner. From the riverbanks, American militia peppered the marines using fowling pieces snatched from above their fireplaces. Cannonballs fired from the American batteries splashed dangerously close. The British returned fire, then retreated down the river. Elkton had been saved by a determined and well-planned defense. Other areas would not be so lucky. A few days later, the British would take out their frustrations at Cecil Furnace in Cecil County, destroying the iron works and sixty-eight cannons made there.

Decades after the attack on Elkton, Thomas J. Sample, who grew up in a stone house next to the gun battery at Elk Landing, described the events to which he had been an eyewitness as a ten-year-old boy. His recollections were published in the *Cecil Whig* on February 24, 1872.

I remember many of the scenes and incidents of the War of 1812; and particularly how the red-coats beat up our quarters so often in Elkton, while they blockaded the Chesapeake. Often we (the women and children—and some men) took what we could conveniently carry and fled for safety. One afternoon after the battery (as we called it) was erected at the Landing (just outside the front door of Sample's boyhood home on the Little Elk Creek) and the good men and brave were there to meet the foe, very many of the women and children were collected at the creek north of the town, awaiting the result of the approach of barges, two men came sneaking by—John and Jim Anderson—and the women opened on them a fire of ridicule, which was very severe, but they kept on, observing the adage, 'He that runs away, may live to fight another day.'

The British fleet lay in the bay, down about Pool's Island and Speutia Island, and from thence they sent marauding parties in barges up the Sassafras, Susquehanna and Elk rivers, robbing hen-roosts, firing private property, and turning up Jack generally. They thus destroyed ware-houses and schooners at Frenchtown, where we had an unfinished fort. They also destroyed Havre de Grace. I saw the smoke at Elkton of the burning property. They essayed to reach Elkton, but finding a Chevaux-de-frise—the iron chain—across the river, and the little battery at the Landing ready to receive them, they retreated, remembering that discretion was the better part of valor. They were a wretched, cowardly set of marauders, going only to those points which were unprotected.

Judge Sample also noted that when the British attacked Baltimore the next year, townspeople in Elkton could "distinctly hear the bombardment of Fort McHenry."

Thomas Sample was not the only local eyewitness with harsh words for the British. Andrew Hall was captain of the 30th Maryland Regiment that took part in the defense of the small town. On November 13, 1813, he described the wartime situation along the Chesapeake Bay in a letter to his brother and sister who had moved to the Ohio frontier.

The times in these parts has been trobelsom. Our waters has been peluted with the English since last Spring and is yet. Thair blockading all our seport towns which causes marchendise of all sorts to be very high espeshaly shoogers and salt . . . On the 26th Aprile we had orders for marching. The meliche not being armed we was in a confused state and on the 28th the British landed at Frenchtown too miles below Elckton and set it on fyer, and consumed it to ashes and would have destroyed Elckton if it had not been they got cowed by the shot of one cannon ball from a small batrey thrown up at the land on (Elk Landing) which proved to have a good effect on them . . . it caused them to retreat by the time the meliche was pretty well collected with a number of armes. They then fell off down the river till the forth day of May, they attempted a landing at Claverde grass (Havre de Grace) under a heavy cannonading on both sides. As they had the greatest force they suckseedid in landing and set fyer to the town and several small vessels that was there and from there to Cull furnes (Principio Furnace—which made cannons) and consumed the whole to ashes. This I was an eye witness to myself. They then fell down the bay till below Anapolis which they continued there and destroyed several small towns. A part of the regiment was caled to Baltimore expecting they would make an etempt there they was caled on for six months but they were discharged at the end of too months. There was several of the neibors and one of my sones at Baltimore. They complean much of bad usage and not annuf to eat allowed them. We think the times here bad annuf althow not so hard as you have fronteers I suppose. I am afraid the next year will be worse in these parts if possible thow I expect we will be prepared for them. Much better again their next visit to us. Got send they may all sinck to the bottom before they ever set their foot on our land again.

These British raids were extremely disruptive to business and family life. Citizen-soldiers such as Captain Hall's neighbors and son, who turned out to defend Baltimore, were rewarded with "bad usage and not annuf to eat allowed them." For the captain and his family, unfortunately, the war would go on for another year.

Elk Landing, the port referred to by Judge Sample and Captain Hall, was largely forgotten during the march of time. The old Stone House where Judge Sample grew up stands beside Little Elk Creek but just a few years ago was in danger of collapsing. The Hollingsworth House, the manor home built in the 1700s by the powerful Hollingsworth family, was as careworn as an old work boot after a series of tenant farmers. Miraculously, the old houses were untouched by vandals, perhaps because the big house is within view of the local sheriff's office. The sixty acres that remain of the once vast estate are secluded, surrounded by rivers and marsh. It is easy to step back in time when visiting there.

What survived of the historic plantation might have languished but in 1999 the town of Elkton bought the property and handed the site over to the Historic Elk Landing Foundation. With nearly two million dollars in grants and private donations, the foundation has begun restoring the site and documenting its past. Ultimately, Elk Landing will become a sixteen-million-dollar living history center where local residents, students and tourists will learn about the past.

To create this center, the history of the site must be carefully documented. Written records don't give the whole picture, so historians are also searching the fields for clues to the past and insights into what happened there during the British attack.

On the first day of March at Elk Landing, the sun was out but the landscape was brown and wintry. Marsh grass waved in the wind like old, bony fingers. A stray dog wandered out of the woods, looked me over, then slipped back into the brush as silently as a wolf. Time itself seemed to have forgotten this lonely spot.

At first, I had not been able to find archaeologist Dwayne Pickett, but I finally spotted him in the distance, stalking back and forth across the stubble of last year's corn. Dotted across the cornfield were yellow marker flags or "pin" flags, the kind that are common at construction sites.

Mention 1812 archaeology in the mid-Atlantic region and Pickett's name invariably pops up. I don't know what I was expecting—maybe Indiana Jones?—but Pickett looked more like he was dressed for a weekend project in the backyard than for exploring the secrets of the past. There was certainly no bullwhip or battered leather jacket in sight. He wore a gray sweatshirt, baseball cap, work boots and blue jeans with a dusting of dirt at the knees. At thirty-six, he looked a bit young—too young, at least, for someone who made his living delving into history.

Pickett was generous with his time and obviously enthusiastic about the project he had undertaken at Elk Landing. He explained that he was trying to determine where future digs should take place by doing a surface sampling of the grounds. He also hoped that an area might turn up with a scattering of artifacts that had been overlooked, maybe hinting at where a cooper shop or an outdoor kitchen once stood.

"Basically, we're just trying to get an idea of what's happening here over the years," Pickett said. "We're just looking for artifact concentrations."

That's where all those pin flags came into play. When I arrived, Pickett had been pacing off distances between the flags. These markers had been pushed into the ground every thirty feet in all directions, a large grid. At each flag, Pickett and his assistant planned to undertake a shovel test. They would dig down twelve to eighteen inches, then dump the soil into a sifter, a wood frame about two-feet square with wire mesh across the bottom.

Maryland had been in a year-long drought, making the archaeologists' work easier. The dusty soil fell away and left behind stones, sticks and historical rubble. With luck, they would find American Indian pottery shards, bits of glass, a musket ball. By the time they finished, they had dug 392 of these shovel tests across the property. Each hole took ten or fifteen minutes to dig, screen, collect any artifacts, take notes and fill the hole back in. In the previous five days before I visited, Pickett and his crew had dug 150 holes. Based on what was found during the shovel test phase, Pickett would do various three-foot square digs to try to locate more objects.

The cornfield had been stingy with its artifacts. Pickett speculated that over the years, most of the arrowheads and larger American Indian artifacts had been picked up by a procession of farmers. What Pickett did find were pottery fragments and bits of stone chipped away in the process of making arrowheads.

"The subsoil is intact but the layers above have been mixed together by plowing and thus artifacts from different time periods are mixed as well," Pickett lamented.

The task of cataloging the items fell to director Christy Groben. Her field lab consisted of a card table set up on the front porch of the Hollingsworth House. There, she used a toothbrush and pan of water to scrub the muddy objects found during the shovel tests.

"A lot of the things they dig up here are the trash items of their day," Groben explained. Some of the objects included buttons, glass, pottery and even a bone-handled toothbrush.

The oldest artifacts were from American Indians who used this tiny peninsula as a jumping off point for trading or food-gathering expeditions down the Chesapeake Bay. Indian burial grounds have even been found within sight of the landing.

Groben showed off a few bits of Indian pottery made of local clay. These were decorated by wrapping twine made of grasses around the wet clay. Centuries later, the lines cut by the twine were visible in the fragments. Groben estimated the pottery dated anywhere from 300 BC to 1600 AD, right about the time the first Europeans arrived. The artifacts were meticulously packaged into plastic bags and Groben recorded where they had been found.

These enthusiastic young archaeologists were a lot like the characters in Michael Crichton's novel, *Timeline*. They obviously enjoyed their work a great deal, especially when something unusual turned up.

As Pickett stood nearly knee-deep in a hole and field archaeologist Keith Heinrich shook a sifter in his big arms, they gleefully shared the story of how they found a glass eyeball at the site. Just as they were doing at that moment, Pickett was shoveling while Heinrich sifted, leaving the historical rubble strewn on the wire mesh. "There it was staring back at me," Heinrich said of the eyeball. "Wow. It kind of took me by surprise."

Glass eyes aside, most of the items found have been domestic artifacts, including rusty nails, buttons, bits of pottery. Military artifacts have been few and far between. A couple of three-pound cannonballs have turned up at the site of the battery that both Judge Sample and Captain Hall wrote about, which helps confirm its location.

According to Pickett, the lack of musket balls and bayonets confirms that the fight here during 1813 was simply a skirmish. Pickett said the situation at Elk Landing is very different from a Civil War battlefield where firing lines can be determined by the string of musket balls dropped by nervous soldiers in the heat of combat, like seeds planted all in a row.

Not all the treasures at Elk Landing came from ground. Barely two weeks after Pickett and his team of archaeologists finished their dig, a volunteer going through boxes of old documents from the Hollingsworth House found a letter signed by John Quincy Adams and another from President Thomas Jefferson discussing the importance of freedom of religion. An appraiser from Christie's auction house in New York would estimate the Jefferson letter's value at more than $700,000.

Even if a large number of battlefield artifacts did not turn up at Elk Landing, Pickett and Heinrich were enthusiastic about the site for the simple reason that it was unspoiled by development. These two have been all over the state of Maryland mapping 1812 sites. They noted that not much has been done to preserve 1812 history statewide. Many sites have been paved over. Few have historical markers. "It's kind of disheartening how little has been saved," Heinrich said.

Both agreed that the lack of preservation effort might come from the fact that most Marylanders don't know much about their 1812 history. Pickett grew up in Montgomery County near Rockville but never learned a great deal about the War of 1812 in school. His class took a field trip to Fort McHenry to learn about the Star-Spangled Banner, and that's as far as the history lesson went. Only when he became an archaeologist did he learn so much about the war. "Wow," he recalled himself saying at the time. "I didn't know any of this stuff had happened."

Heinrich stated the archaeologists' opinion about why War of 1812 history wasn't more popular. "The Americans' failures at the beginning of the war don't make a really good historical tale. They would turn tail and run. That doesn't make for a good, romantic story. Also, in the Revolutionary War we were fighting for our freedom. During the War of 1812 we were fighting against trade restrictions. That's not very glamorous. Of course, it did establish us as an independent nation."

Heinrich said the lack of attention given the War of 1812 in the upper Chesapeake Bay region also has to do with the scope and scale of the war. Besides Fort McHenry, which he called the best-interpreted 1812 site in Maryland, and the burning of Washington, most of the conflict was on a smaller scale. "Here, they burned Havre de Grace, they burned Frenchtown and all the little towns nobody knows anything about," he said. "It's about time that people got more interested."

The digs conducted by Pickett and Heinrich at Elk Landing did turn up a few clues about the war. Earlier, the two had conducted a dig near where accounts of the day claimed the gun battery had been located. They surveyed an area measuring roughly thirty square feet. First, a metal detector was used and each "hit" was marked with a flag. The archaeologists dug down at each flag and sifted through the soil, with the position of each excavated shovel test being documented with photographs and a Global Positioning Satellite reading.

They found nails and other modern metal objects, but also one item that was unmistakably from the 1813 fight—a three-pound iron cannonball. A similar cannonball had been found nearby in the 1930s and is now in the care of the county historical society.

The more recent discovery made headlines in local newspapers. All these years later, the British attack was still making news.

6

Secrets of the Past
Documenting History at Elk Landing and the
Maryland Archaeological Research Facility

Digging is not the only way to document the history of an 1812 site. Technology has provided ever more high-tech methods for studying the past. Computer analysis, Global Positioning Systems, metal detectors, side-scan sonar for mapping sunken ships and even remote-controlled exploration robots are new tools being used by historians.

One such method was being put to use on a January morning at Elk Landing. A chainsaw buzzed in the winter air, slicing through thick timbers taken from the Stone House. The silence after the roar of the saw was sudden and complete. The winter landscape felt timeless, surrounded by these old buildings beside the slow-moving Little Elk Creek. A rime of crusty white snow, thawed and frozen again, covered the brown thatch of last year's grass. This could have been 2004 or 1812 or even 1700—all we had to do was trade in our polyester fleece for buckskin, wool and fur.

Records leave no doubt that the Stone House existed during the 1813 fight to save Elkton from British torches. But just how old *was* the building? Some local historians claimed the house dated to the late 1600s, when Swedish settlers established a trading post at Elk Landing to barter with the Susquehannock Indians.

The archaeologists had done their work. Now it was time for another kind of historical research. At first glance, it looked as if someone was cutting up the ancient timbers to fuel a woodstove. The chainsaw was actually the first step in an advanced dating process.

"It's called dendrochronology," said Bill Callahan, bundled against the cold. He explained that this dating process relies on studying the growth rings of trees. The rings vary in width according to growing conditions during any particular year. Drought results in a narrow ring, while a rainy year appears as a wide band. Tree growth for the region has been well documented over the centuries, enabling scientists to create a timeline using these ring patterns. Timbers taken from the Stone House would be analyzed to determine the year they were cut.

Helping Callahan were James Wollon, preservation architect for Elk Landing, and Josh Brown, the construction manager. They walked among the timbers collected from the Stone House and Hollingsworth House during renovation work, sizing them up. Centuries-old axe cuts marked where the logs had been shaped by settlers. Bits of bark clung to the timbers, strewn on the frozen ground like so many bones at a crime scene.

Like two detectives, Wollon and Callahan examined the evidence. From time to time, Brown fired up his chainsaw to cut an inch-thick cross section of a timber. Other samples were taken using a long drill bit that removed a pencil-thin core.

"How 'bout this one here?" Callahan asked, studying an oak timber more than a foot thick.

"That's from the inner edge against the house wall," Wollon answered.

Callahan nodded and chalked a number on the beam. He moved on to a log gone spongy with decay. "This is poplar.

It's probably not going to give us anything."

The timbers revealed other clues, such as traces of charred wood from a documented 1848 fire, mortise holes that showed a particular beam had been recycled from somewhere else on the site, and hand-forged nails that bristled on the surface of another log.

"We should be able to date this," Callahan said. "A tree grows in relationship to its environment. All types of things play a role in its growth."

The samples collected at Elk Landing were analyzed at the Lamont-Doherty Tree-Ring Lab in Nyack, New York. There, the sections of timber were highly polished so that the growth rings could be measured to within .0001 mm. By the end of July, the results of the $3,500 study were back. The tree rings revealed that the timbers for the Stone House were cut in 1783, possibly 1782. While not as old as some had hoped, the house had seen its share of history.

Much further down the Chesapeake Bay, on the site of another War of 1812 battlefield, a different kind of historical research was taking place at the Maryland Archaeological Conservation Laboratory. This facility is one of the most high-tech archaeological research centers in the United States.

The lab houses everything from American Indian stone artifacts to 1812 cannons. The 38,000 square-foot lab, built in 1998 on the shore of the Patuxent River in a relatively rural area, may be one of the state's best-kept secrets. The lab is part of Jefferson Patterson Park and Museum, a state-owned property in Calvert County. At this spot in 1814, Joshua Barney took on the Royal Navy in what would become known as the battle of St. Leonard's Creek.

"We're something of a cross between a factory and a laboratory," explained Michael Smolek, director of the research facility.

Smolek brings visitors through the front door into a world where artifacts long buried in the chaotic muck and mire of history are sorted out and studied. He compared the lab to a factory where the "raw materials" of history enter at one end of the building and eventually become preserved artifacts ready for display in museums or exhibits.

Most of the artifacts in the lab don't come from scientific digs but are unearthed during the construction of roads and buildings across Maryland. Of the more than seven million artifacts logged in here, Smolek said, fully a quarter of the objects were unearthed during state highway projects. When the objects arrive, they are placed in special, sealed storage rooms. Along with clues to history, objects often come with pests such as cockroaches and silverfish. "It hopefully gets more pest-free as it moves," he said.

First stop on the tour was a spotless "clean room." Large stainless steel tables—each representing an archaeological research project in progress—were spread throughout the spacious room. The room's large windows face north like they would in an artist's studio, Smolek explained, because northern light gives a fuller spectrum of colors.

Along one wall was a bank of shallow steel drawers. Smolek slid one open to reveal several pottery shards. "That's all eighteenth and seventeenth century stuff," he said, then moved to another drawer containing primitive stone objects. He picked one up. "That's at least three thousand years old. It's the handle for a stone bowl." Yet another drawer held a clay pipe and a stone axe head.

All these items are being cataloged and stored for further study or use in museums. Other artifacts were displayed in glass cases visible from the hallway. These included bits of barbed wire and even pieces from a child's doll—items from an African-American homestead that stood near where the lab is now located.

Smolek led the way through the corridors. The ceilings were high and spacious. Glass walls allowed a clear view into the various work areas. Around every corner was something unique, including an exhibit of artwork by staff members.

Inside one room, Smolek popped an x-ray onto a light box like you would expect to see in a doctor's office. Instead of bones, the x-ray revealed the ghostly image of a flintlock pistol from the 1700s. He explained that the pistol was found by a worker during the construction of the Camden Yards baseball stadium in downtown Baltimore.

The x-ray showed rust inside the lock mechanism, which meant the pistol would have to be taken apart and cleaned, something conservators had not wanted to do. Smolek noted that the pistol posed a particular challenge because it was made of wood, iron and copper, which all "want to be conserved in a different way." The industrial-sized 320-KV x-ray apparatus occupies a massive lead-lined vault in an isolated section of the building. The doors alone weigh thousands of pounds.

Film flapped as Smolek put up another x-ray. This image was of the copper, lead and wood acorn sculpture taken from atop the statehouse dome in Annapolis during renovation work. Beneath more than twenty layers of paint, the x-ray revealed that eighteen-century workers had scratched their names into the metal.

"What a treasure for a genealogist," he said, explaining that this historical graffiti places an artisan at a particular time and place.

The facility was packed with similar items, all with a story to tell. A history buff would describe some artifacts as treasures, although you might not know what you were looking at without a little help. One such treasure was the helm of the *CSS Alabama*, rescued from the ocean waters off

Cherbourg, France, and now the property of the United States Navy. In a black and white photograph nearby, Confederate Navy Captain Raphael Semmes stands on the deck of his famous ship with that very helm visible in the background. It is a well-known photograph of Semmes, who looks dashing in his long sea coat. To see an actual piece of the ship from that photograph is enough to leave some visitors speechless. "We had some Civil War re-enactors come in here and practically kneel on the floor," Smolek said.

The other object of note in this finishing room is a one-log canoe found in Trappe Creek on Maryland's Eastern Shore. After the wood is preserved and the canoe reassembled, the centuries-old vessel will go on display at the Chesapeake Bay Museum in St. Michaels.

When it comes to War of 1812 artifacts, Smolek offers a few anecdotes that might go under the heading of a mini-lecture entitled, "Is this thing loaded?"

Cannonballs from 1812 pop up with regularity in the Chesapeake Bay region. Most of the smaller cannonballs, like those three-pounders found at Elk Landing, are solid iron and relatively safe unless you happen to drop one on your foot. The dangerous cannonballs have a hollow core filled with gunpowder. These are the "bombs bursting in air" variety.

Black powder is very unstable and can be explosive years later, even after being deep underwater. Smolek stressed that caution is needed when handling old military ordnance and ammunition. There is no sense in becoming a casualty of a war that ended nearly 200 years ago.

Smolek recounted the story of one Marylander who found a cannonball in a creek and brought it home, then mentioned his find to Smolek. His advice was for the man to carry it out very carefully, put it in the shade far from the house, and call the bomb squad. He also shared a couple of horror stories about people who had old cannonballs rolling around behind the seat of a pickup truck or sitting on a mantel where an explosion could handily take out a whole family gathered in front of the fireplace.

The cannons that hurled these cannonballs were being salvaged in another area of the lab. Cannons are designated by the weight of the cannonball they fired. Some of the 1798 eighteen-pounders being preserved were off the *USS Constellation* in Baltimore. "They probably would have been used during the War of 1812," Smolek said.

Another War of 1812 cannon being worked on at the lab was pressed into service by the Confederate States of America during the Civil War. A massive collar was added at the cannon's base and the bore of the barrel received rifling—adaptations for more advanced Civil War-era munitions. According to Smolek, the Confederacy often recycled 1812 cannons because the rebellious states' iron works could not produce enough new guns for the war.

Nearby, an 1812-era six-pounder off a British ship, *HMS Nimrod*, stewed in a water-filled vat. The *Nimrod* ran aground in Long Island Sound during the war and threw off several guns to lighten its load enough to float free. The cannon was loaded when it was recovered. Conservators removed two cannonballs and a linen-covered sack of black powder—but only after determining that seawater had neutralized the explosive.

Electrical wires ran down into the water. Smolek explained that the mild charge was removing the oxygen and hydrogen from the iron, causing the water to bubble slightly. The process gets rid of the salts that have been absorbed during nearly 200 years in the sea. Unless the salt is removed, the iron will begin to flake or "spall."

Another vat held what vaguely resembled a giant slingshot made from the fork of a tree. The object was actually a dogshear, or support for the curved sides of a wooden ship.

This particular dogshear was found underwater near Annapolis at the former Stewart Shipyard, which was burned during the Revolutionary War.

To preserve this historic item, conservators placed it in a vat of polyethylene glycol, a liquid wax that dissolves in water and is absorbed by wood. The dogshear was soft and spongy to the touch from underwater bacteria. The wax slowly replaces the water in the wood. Once that occurred, the dogshear would be placed in a giant freeze-dry machine and the temperature reduced to −250 degrees in a vacuum. The dogshear could then be safely displayed outside its vat.

This section of the lab was equipped with some serious industrial equipment. A crane was available to move heavy objects such as dogshears and cannons. A series of drains carries off any spilled chemicals to holding tanks, either to be reused or disposed of safely. There were two freeze-drying units, the larger measuring four feet by twelve feet, the biggest in the United States.

Last stop on the tour was a room that resembled a warehouse, with storage crates stacked to the ceiling. I had the creepy sensation of having walked into the scene at the end of the 1980s adventure film *Raiders of the Lost Ark* in which the crated Ark of the Covenant is hidden in a sprawling government warehouse. Inside these crates were future projects, including the entire office of longtime Maryland state comptroller Louis L. Goldstein, neatly boxed up and awaiting an appropriate home.

The wreckage of an 1828 ship known as *Columbus* was spread upon archival plastic pallets on the floor. Weathered iron pistons and shafts from the ship's steam engine resembled the blackened bones of a dinosaur. The 178-foot vessel caught fire in 1850 and sank after burning to the waterline. The remains in the warehouse were of its engine, the oldest marine steam engine in the United States.

Smolek pointed out that in 1814, when war was raging on the Chesapeake Bay, all boats relied upon sails. By 1828 there was steam power, rendering obsolete the age of sail that had lasted for thousands of years. He compared the changeover to the leap from manual typewriters to laptop computers. "Imagine going from sail to steam in fourteen years. It was truly amazing."

The fact that ships in the War of 1812 relied on sails adds romance to the sea captains and privateers of the day. Something about steam power seems far more industrial and impersonal.

Later, in Smolek's office in an old house beside the lab, we talked about the lab's projects and local history. Many of Smolek's duties involve administration, but it's clear he loves to be involved as closely as possible in all the center's archaeological projects. Smolek also enjoys sailing and our conversation touched on everything from primitive navigation using the stars to who might have been the first Europeans to reach North America. From a sailor's perspective, he lamented the fact that most twenty-first century Americans don't take note of their natural surroundings.

"Most people don't pay attention to the night sky anymore," he said, then fired a question at me. "Do you know what phase the moon is in?"

"It's waxing."

"Very good," he said, surprised but clearly pleased.

I was glad I had been outside enjoying the clear autumn sky the night before. It seemed to me that Smolek probably kept his staff on their toes by popping questions at them.

Our conversation came around to the War of 1812. He noted that the pleasant farmland of the park had been touched by war and devastation during 1812. "People died here," he said. "People's homes were burned. It gives you some perspective that our nation has been through trials before and we'll overcome them.

"The problem with the War of 1812 is that it's not the Founding, you don't have that cornerstone of history in the classroom with the tri-cornered hats and all that, and you don't have the Civil War images, so it's kind of hard to relate to," he said, noting that photography wouldn't be invented for years to come. "Then again, if you don't consider the burning of the nation's capital and the writing of *The Star-Spangled Banner* important, then what is?"

7

The Burning of Havre de Grace

How a lone Irishman took on the Royal Navy

On a sunny May afternoon nearly 189 years to the day since it was sacked and burned by the British, the town of Havre de Grace was captured again.

"Die you English dogs!" shouted a soldier in an elegant blue uniform. His flintlock musket fired and white smoke rolled across the battlefield.

From the Susquehanna River, a motley crew of attackers swarmed toward town. Some wore red coats, others the blue of British sailors. They snapped off a few shots at the American force taking refuge in a "fort" made of stockade fencing that looked suspiciously as if it might have come from Home Depot. However, the sharpened sticks or *abatis* jutting from the ground at an angle and ending about throat-height appeared very realistic and nasty. Not something you would want to impale yourself on at a dead run, even at a re-enactment.

"Boo to the British!" yelled one of the spectators sitting on a straw bale and watching from behind a streamer of yellow caution tape that ringed the battlefield.

The Americans fired a ragged volley from their makeshift fort and two of the fattest attackers flopped down to play dead, then lay wheezing as the attack pressed on. "They just didn't want to run all that way," one woman in the crowd wisecracked, and laughter rippled through the spectators.

As re-enactments go, it was not terribly realistic, but with a little imagination it was possible to envision what the attack early on the morning of May 4, 1813, was like as the British landed to ransack and burn the town. In recent years Havre de Grace has been holding an annual re-enactment on the anniversary of the town's destruction at British hands.

It became clear from watching the British recapture Havre de Grace that the difference between War of 1812 re-enacting and Civil War re-enacting is like the contrast between golf and rugby. Civil War re-enactors tend to be an intense bunch when it comes to their mock battles, while the older War of 1812 crowd takes a more casual approach. They stroll toward the enemy where Civil War soldiers would be charging ahead and screaming a rebel yell. This difference continued over into the general appearance of the 1812 troops. The sixty or so re-enactors at Havre de Grace were mostly duffers in their fifties or beyond. Some of the more fit and trim men looked sharp in their tailored uniforms, while others were so well-fed that in a real battle they would have made invitingly large targets. They were all good sports to be on the battlefield in their scratchy wool uniforms for the benefit of the crowd that had come to watch and learn about the War of 1812.

Most of the town's defenders in 1813 actually were older men. Back in the early 1800s all males between the ages of eighteen and forty-five were required to have a firearm and be familiar with its use. All the younger men from Havre de Grace were off defending Baltimore, so this left the over-the-hill crowd back home to stand against crack troops as best they could.

The town was put to the torch in 1813 with a substantial property loss. The attack was surprisingly bloodless, probably because most of the fifty or sixty American militia soldiers ran after a few shots were exchanged. According to Vincent Vaise, a national park ranger from Fort McHenry who narrated the re-enactment, the British lost three killed and two wounded. One American was killed when he was beheaded by a Congreve rocket.

"You can imagine how demoralizing that must have been to his comrades," Vaise said. "We couldn't recreate those rockets here today, but they were truly the terror weapons of their day."

Vaise made more than one reference to terrorism, making the connection between September 11, 2001, and Admiral Cockburn's attacks on the Chesapeake Bay. "The attack on Havre de Grace may seem like a long time ago but after September 11 the idea of an invasion by an enemy seems far more current," Vaise told the crowd. "The emotions felt by the people here were very much like the ones we felt upon hearing of the attack on our nation."

Today, Havre de Grace is a pleasant waterfront town at the point where the mighty Susquehanna River empties into the Chesapeake Bay. The river begins its 444-mile journey at Cooperstown, New York, home of the Baseball Hall of Fame.

Havre de Grace was given its French name by the Marquis de Lafayette, who declared that the town should be called "beautiful harbor." After the Revolutionary War, the streets were renamed for heroes and battlefields: Washington, Revolution, Concord, and so on. A bustling downtown with shops and restaurants is surrounded by several stately homes. All in all, the town recovered from British devastation quite nicely, while other places along the bay never seemed to regain momentum after being put to the torch.

Havre de Grace's main attraction is the waterfront. There are marinas and a boardwalk that provides a nice place to stroll while taking in the scenic vistas. One end of this popular boardwalk is anchored by an old lighthouse known as

Concord Point Light.

Don't expect a lighthouse as tall and windswept as those guarding the rocky coasts of Maine or the shoals of Cape Hatteras. This one was scaled to the Chesapeake Bay rather than the sea. Built in 1827, Concord Point Light is thirty-six feet tall, with whitewashed walls nearly four feet thick at the base. The structure is built of granite from the nearby town of Port Deposit just upriver on the Susquehanna.

Standing at the water's edge, it is worth taking a moment to get one's bearings. Just visible in the haze to the southeast are the cliffs of Turkey Point at Elk Neck State Park. Admiral Cockburn's fleet would have been anchored off Turkey Point and was probably just discernable from town if the weather was clear.

A monument at the base of the lighthouse features a badly weathered cannon set into a chunk of Port Deposit granite. A bronze plaque honors John O'Neill for his defense of the city. It adds that his daughter, Matilda, obtained her father's release from Cockburn's ship after he was captured. Cockburn supposedly gave her a gold snuffbox. The plaque also mentions that the citizens of Philadelphia later presented O'Neill with a sword for his heroism. Another historical marker at the water's edge notes that O'Neill manned a gun battery on high ground nearby.

O'Neill's stubborn defense of Havre de Grace is one of the town's great legends. With the British prowling on the bay, there had been a general alarm on May 2 and the local militia turned out, but the citizens' martial fervor quickly waned when the British did not appear.

The attack early on May 3 caught the townspeople by surprise. According to an account published in the *Baltimore Sun* in 1959 and written by Catherine O'Neill Gunther, great-granddaughter of the man who became the hero of the battle, the British launched their attack with a fifteen-minute bombardment by nineteen barges. Rockets exploded and shells burst overhead. That terrifying show of firepower was enough to discourage any serious resistance from the local militia.

O'Neill, however, was not scared off so easily. He was a nailmaker in town and a militia lieutenant. O'Neill, born in Ireland in 1769, most likely had a genetic hatred of the British.

After the other defenders ran away, O'Neill single-handedly manned the artillery battery near where the lighthouse now stands. According to his great-granddaughter, it was called the "Potato Battery" because of the size of the iron shot fired by the two six-pound and one nine-pound guns.

As rockets burst around him and grapeshot clawed the air, O'Neill kept on firing at the British until he was injured when his cannon recoiled before he could get out of the way. Undaunted, O'Neill limped back to town and tried to rally a few of the militia. He used his musket as a crutch, stopping now and then to take a shot at the British.

O'Neill gave the following account in a letter,

I retreated down to town, and joined Mr. Barnes, of the nail manufactory, with a musket, and fired on the barges while we had ammunition, and then retreated to the common, where I kept waving my hat to the militia who had run away, to come to our assistance, but they proved cowardly and would not come back.

His somewhat madcap defense may have saved him from being killed outright by a British bayonet. The Redcoats took him prisoner and carried him back to Admiral Cockburn's flagship, *HMS Maidstone.*

The British looted the town and set houses on fire. About forty of the town's sixty houses burned to the ground.

American accounts describe a nightmarish scene in which the British smash everything in sight. The invaders shot pigs and other animals, leaving them dead or maimed in the streets. The British "outraged and insulted" women and children. Stagecoaches were destroyed, their horses cruelly crippled. The British even shattered the windows of the town's Episcopal church, stopping short of setting it ablaze. The Redcoats spared the home of Commodore John Rodgers, who was busy fighting the Royal Navy for control of the Great Lakes. His home was left standing as a matter of professional courtesy and serves today as a barbershop.

Spoils of war were seized. Sailors and marines dismantled several fine stages and loaded them on barges. British troops robbed travelers on the road between Baltimore and Philadelphia.

The *Niles Weekly Register* newspaper railed against Admiral Cockburn's actions, trumpeting,

> Wanton outrage!
> Many fled from their burning houses almost in a state of nudity, carrying in their arms their children, clothes, &c.
>
> The ruins of Havre de Grace shall stand as a monument to British cruelty . . . The villain-deed has roused the honest indignation of every man—no one pretends to justify or excuse it. It has knit the people into a common bond for vengeance on the incendiaries.
>
> . . . If admiral Cockburn has his secret agents in Baltimore, we hope they may faithfully communicate to him the events of that day: and let him, glory, if he can, in the effect that his barbarous conduct to poor Havre de Grace has produced. The conflagration of that village purified party in Baltimore . . . For, or, against the English, is the only touchstone.

The attack on Havre de Grace only served to further galvanize Maryland residents against the marauders. I even came across a bit of anonymous doggerel from the early 1800s that lambasted the British and Admiral Cockburn in particular.

That impious wretch with coward voice decreed,
Defenceless domes and hallow'd fanes to dust;
Beheld, with seeming smile, the wounded bleed,
And spurr'd his bands to rapine, blood, and lust.
Vain was the widow's, vain the orphan's cry,
To touch his feelings or to sooth his rage -
Vain the fair drop that roll'd from beauty's eye,
Vain the dumb grief of supplicating age.

On board Admiral Cockburn's flagship, the future looked grim for Lieutenant O'Neill. Any subject or former subject of the crown who took up arms against the king was considered a traitor, subject to death. O'Neill's teen-age daughter intervened, rowing out to Cockburn's flagship to plead for her father's life. He gave the girl the snuffbox and at least one account has Cockburn and O'Neill then getting drunk together on Irish whiskey, but that seems highly unlikely. Cockburn might have been a sucker for a pretty face, but he was not known for his hospitality or for mixing with the lower classes of Americans and Irishmen.

There might have been a less romantic, more practical reason why O'Neill was spared. The American government had promised to retaliate if any naturalized citizens were hanged. A letter Cockburn received from General Henry Miller, the American commander in Baltimore, warned that two British prisoners would be hanged if any harm came to O'Neill. Cockburn might not have been willing to see if the general would make good on his threat.

O'Neill became the town's most celebrated citizen. When Concord Point Light was built, the local hero of the War of 1812 was made the lighthouse keeper for the rest of his life. The job also came with a comfortable stone house for the keeper. O'Neill died in 1837 and freed his three slaves in his will. The job of light keeper passed to his son, John Jr., who held the post until his own death in 1863. This sinecure then passed to John Jr.'s daughter, Esther, until 1878, and then to her brother, Henry O'Neill. When Henry died in 1919, the job fell to his son, Harry O'Neill. O'Neills might still be carrying up the whale oil and lighting the lamp if the federal government had not installed an automatic electric light in the late 1920s and eliminated the light keeper's post.

The attack on Havre de Grace may have been provoked by the sight of a massive United States flag flying over the town. At the conclusion of the re-enactment, a replica of the Star-Spangled Banner that flew at Fort McHenry was unfurled. The spectators, so eager to touch a part of the flag, rushed forward to grab the flag's edge. Standing shoulder to shoulder they stretched the huge banner out to catch the May sunshine. Park Ranger Vaise had brought out the flag to make a point. "We still feel strongly about the flag today, and after the attack on September 11 the flag was a symbol that helped bring Americans together," he said.

"Out on their ships, the British said, 'How dare they fly that flag and flaunt the symbol of their upstart nation!' It outraged and taunted the British and probably led to some of the excessive damage done during the attack here. They were truly chagrined to see that flag," Vaise said. The fate of the huge Havre de Grace flag is not known, although it is likely the British seized it as a war trophy.

"More than a year later and fifty miles south of here,

another huge flag would fly over the city of Baltimore," Vaise continued. "Only this time the British would not be successful in their attack. It would be an American victory and that flag would become a national symbol."

8

Making the Flag
An independent Baltimore widow creates a national symbol

The story of America's most famous flag begins in the summer of 1814, when the first stitches of the Star-Spangled Banner were sewn. This was the enormous flag that flew as the defeated British fleet sailed away from Baltimore on September 14, 1814. The British could not resist firing a few parting shots, tearing holes in the fabric.

The huge flag was also an inspiration to an amateur poet who witnessed the battle. *By dawn's early light,* Francis Scott Key jotted down a few verses of what would become the national anthem. The flag that inspired the poem would forever be known as *The Star-Spangled Banner.*

The history of that flag, of how if came to be made by an independent-minded widow, begins at The Star-Spangled Banner House on East Pratt Street. The brick row house is located just a few blocks beyond Baltimore's bustling Inner Harbor attractions, but on a July day with the temperature near one hundred degrees and Maryland's infamous humidity draped over the city like a wet blanket, only a handful of people had made the walk to this quiet historical spot.

"It's a war that you don't hear a lot about unless you live in Baltimore," said tour guide Ellie Marine, adding that there had been a slight increase in the number of visitors to the flag house since the terrorist attacks.

In 1812, this modest city row house was the home of Mary Young Pickersgill, a successful flag maker and quiet patriot. Pickersgill was a rarity at a time when business pursuits were very much a man's domain. Marine led our small group of visitors through the house where the resourceful Mrs. Pickersgill managed to carve out a middleclass living.

When her husband died on a business trip to England in 1805, she was left to support herself. By 1812, she had a large household that included her elderly mother, fourteen-year-old daughter Caroline, a female slave, a free African American servant and a young girl apprenticed to her. Aside from the occasional male boarder, the row house was very much a woman's domain.

"The house was located near the harbor and they had a very successful business supplying flags to ships," Marine said. "A flag maker in Baltimore was quite busy if she was good. Every ship owner in Baltimore had his own flag. Also, things like signal flags wear out very quickly and have to be replaced."

Pickersgill inherited her flag-making skills from her mother, Rebecca Young, who made the Grand Union flag that flew over George Washington's headquarters at Valley Forge during the Revolutionary War. You might recognize a picture of it from your grade school history book. The banner featured the same red and white stripes of today's flag but displayed a Union Jack in place of the blue field and white stars.

"That's one of the coincidences of history that you have a mother-daughter flag making team," Marine said. "It's one of those things you'll never see again."

Pickersgill's days were full of hard work. She rose before dawn to stoke the kitchen fire and start the day's cooking, then met with customers and sewed flags. Pickersgill did not know it yet, but the War of 1812 was about to make her famous.

Major George Armistead, commander at Fort McHenry, was the man who first proposed a huge flag for the fort guarding the city's harbor. In a letter to General Sam Smith, military commander of Baltimore, he wrote,

We, sir, are ready at Fort McHenry to defend Baltimore against invading by the enemy. That is to say, we are ready except that we have no suitable ensign to display over the Star Fort and it is my desire to have a flag so large that the British will have no difficulty seeing it from a distance.

A delegation consisting of Armistead, Smith, General John Stricker and Pickersgill's brother-in-law—that old salt Commodore Joshua Barney—soon called on the seamstress. They met in the downstairs dining room, where they sipped tea and discussed the particulars of the flag.

The men wanted an enormous banner measuring thirty feet by forty-two feet. Fifteen stars and fifteen stripes would represent each state of the Union. The stars would be two feet across. The stripes would each be two feet wide, eight red and seven white. For her efforts, Pickersgill would receive $405.90, a sum this savvy businesswoman must have known would barely pay her expenses for the material alone.

According to historians at the flag house, it is likely that Pickersgill donated her labor out of a sense of patriotism. Taking on the job also could have been a matter of professional pride. She might have welcomed the chance to make a flag as prestigious as the one that would fly over Fort McHenry.

To make such a huge flag required a lightweight material; otherwise, it would have been too heavy to fly. Pickersgill settled on a loosely woven fabric known as English wool bunting. She secured 400 yards of it at a cost of one dollar per yard. Ironically, the fabric for the flag came from America's enemy in 1812. Pickersgill was well-connected with sea captains willing to run the blockade and deliver the necessary fabric from England.

"From what we understand, she got the wool bunting while we were at war with England by making a deal with a privateer," Marine said. Obtaining the fabric was only the first obstacle. "Mary finds out very quickly that she has a bit of a problem. She realizes she's going to run out of room in her house. You would find you had two feet of English bunting to go when you ran out of room."

To keep from having to bunch up the fabric and make a mess of the stitching, she moved the project to a brewery where there was room to spread out. Pickersgill did not work on the flag alone, but historians say she did most of the sewing herself.

"She started very early in the morning before anyone else was up and she worked late into the night," Marine said. Pickersgill was already awake when the household stirred to life at about five o'clock and the work of the day began. She toiled on the flag until at least nine in the evening and sometimes past midnight. By the time the flag makers were done, Pickersgill and her assistants had sewn 350,000 stitches. Pickersgill must have been exhausted.

Several years ago, a group of seventy-seven women took seven weeks to sew a replica of the flag. Pickersgill did it in six weeks. Her flag was finished on August 10, 1814. The British attack on Baltimore came just over one month later.

Historians are fairly certain that the flag flying above Fort McHenry for most of the battle was not the actual Star-Spangled Banner. Instead, the fort flew a smaller "storm flag" that had also been made by Pickersgill. The Star-Spangled

Banner was raised toward the end of the fight. One reason for using the storm flag was that a heavy rain fell during most of the battle. Marine pointed out that the rain would have made the full-sized flag so heavy that it might have snapped the flag pole. "Lucky for us it did rain," Marine said. "Many of the bombs fizzled out in the air. Most likely the flag was hit when the British fired their last shots."

During past occasions at the flag house, Marine has donned a gown and mob cap to portray the nineteenth century seamstress. In costume, Marine bears more than a passing resemblance to the round-faced, bespectacled Pickersgill.

Marine spoke enthusiastically, even wistfully, about 1812-era Baltimore. Streets were muddy or dusty, depending on the season. Daily chores included hauling water from City Springs six blocks away. The women of the Pickersgill household were constantly in the kitchen preparing food or heating irons in the large fireplace to smooth the wrinkles out of newly-made flags. "It reflected better on Mary's work if the flags left here neater than her competition," Marine said.

One by one, Marine explained the items in a nineteenth century kitchen. A cast-iron crane was used to hang kettles and pots over the fire. A reflecting oven had a spit for roasting meat, another oven was intended for baking bread. Marine pointed out that the open fire made the kitchen a dangerous place to work. Burns were the second leading cause of death for women. Only childbirth killed more. "We take a lot for granted today," Marine said. "They would no sooner have finished breakfast than it was time to start preparing the main meal of the day. They spent all day cooking."

"Everything back then was so much work!" said a woman from California, who had spent the previous day visiting the original flag at the Smithsonian Institution. "It kind of makes you appreciate TV dinners."

This household of seamstresses enjoyed occasional small pleasures, such as tea or even hot chocolate. Sugar was so valuable it was kept under lock and key. The kitchen might have been the heart of the house, but it was the flag business that kept the larder stocked.

In addition to making flags, Pickersgill also kept a boarder in a second-floor bedroom advertised as a "healthful room" by dint of its three windows that provided ventilation. The boarders were generally sea captains Pickersgill knew, in town for a few weeks or months before their ship set sail again.

"Her mother knew what it was like to keep body and soul together and she passed that ethic on to Mary," Marine said of Pickersgill's upbringing. "In the first quarter of the nineteenth century, there are not many options for women without funds. It's a very hard time if you do not have money."

An awareness of the thin line between the middleclass and poverty likely led Pickersgill to become a social activist. Together with similar-minded women, in 1802 she formed a group to help respectable women whose support systems had crumbled. This often meant widowed young mothers and elderly spinsters. To help those in need, the group founded what was somewhat ponderously called the Impartial Female and Humane Society and Male Free School. "She had seen a lot of women fall through the cracks and left destitute," Marine said.

Mary died in 1857 at age eighty-one. Her legacy survives at the Pickersgill Retirement Community. Begun in the mid-1800s, the facility recently underwent a major renovation, and continues to carry out the work its founder envisioned.

Within days of the British defeat at Baltimore, the flag that had flown over Fort McHenry was famous. The major victory, the flag's massive size and Francis Scott Key's poem were a powerful combination. Thanks to Key, the flag also had a name, the Star-Spangled Banner.

When Armistead gave up his command of Fort McHenry he took the flag with him. Historians say it's likely the former commander was given the flag as a token of thanks.

It wasn't long before the flag began to be diminished by bits and pieces. British cannonballs began the process and the widows of veterans soon joined in. "The widows came and asked if they might have a piece of the flag to bury with their husbands and Major Armistead obliged them," Marine explained.

Visitors and dinner guests received pieces of the flag as souvenirs. At some point, one of the two-foot stars was cut away. Destroying a valued item in the process of admiring it may seem strange today, but such keepsakes were common in the nineteenth century. Confederate hero Robert E. Lee, for example, was besieged by admirers seeking tokens. He sent them locks of his hair or buttons from his uniform. For the flag, the deterioration would continue for nearly a century, until the Star-Spangled Banner passed into the hands of the Smithsonian Institution in 1907.

9

Saving the Flag
A Visit to the Smithsonian Institution

Not much gets past Officer Ira Green. For the last three and a half years, she has stood guard over the dimly-lit room at the Smithsonian Institution that holds one of America's most treasured artifacts. She is a security guard who doubles as an unofficial tour guide, glad to tell anyone what they want to know about the Star-Spangled Banner.

"It looks a lot better now," she said. "It was really beat up before but now it looks at rest."

The first known photograph of the flag, taken by Navy historian George Preble in 1873, shows that the banner's white stripes were already dark with age, its tatters more than apparent.

Older visitors to the Smithsonian may recall seeing the flag on display before it was moved to this sealed room at the Museum of American History. Covered by a replica, the actual flag was revealed under dim lighting for a few minutes every hour. The national anthem played while the flag was on view.

That public display took a further toll on the flag already assaulted by British bombs and nineteenth century souvenir-seekers who had trimmed a full eight feet off its trailing edge. After nearly 200 years, the red stripes had faded to pink. Exhaust drifted in from the streets of Washington and attached itself to the woolen fibers, causing further harm.

In 1999, an $18 million restoration project began to save the historic flag from the ravages of time. Fashion magnate Ralph Lauren, whose designs often incorporate the flag, contributed $10 million to the effort.

The flag was taken down and moved into an atmospherically controlled room. There, conservators lay on their stomachs on thin mattress pads on a mobile steel platform suspended above the horizontal surface of the flag. The 6,000-pound platform can only be moved by hand because there's no electricity involved. Conservators weren't sure how electricity would affect the fabric. Plus, as Officer Green pointed out, there have been fires before at the museum. Eliminating electricity from the flag room reduced the risk of fire.

"We're not trying to restore the flag, we're not trying to make it look the way it did the morning Key saw it," explained Suzanne Thomassen-Krauss, chief conservator for the Star-Spangled Banner Preservation Effort at the Smithsonian. According to Thomassen-Krauss, the goal is to return the flag to the condition it was in when acquired by the Smithsonian in 1907.

Through a large glass wall, visitors can see the conservators work on the flag stitch by stitch. It is not exactly exciting to watch unless you bring a sense of imagination and remember the colorful history involved. On my visit, the flag looked a little sad, its deteriorated state in sharp contrast to the almost medically sterile conditions surrounding it. It reminded me of visiting a very old relative in the hospital and seeing the depressing contrast between leathery, wrinkled skin and crisp, white hospital sheets. Fortunately, Officer Green was there to liven things up. "I love being part of this project," she said. "This is a neat place. I'm still amazed all the time."

Thomassen-Krauss and the other conservators are mainly undoing earlier attempts at preserving the Star-Spangled Banner. The flag became part of the museum's collection in 1912 when the loan became a permanent gift to the Smithsonian from Eben Appleton, a descendant of Fort McHenry's Major Armistead. Incredible as it sounds today, the flag at one point was actually hung outside from the walls of the Smithsonian's original "castle" building on the National Mall. In 1914, renowned flag restorer Amelia Fowler was hired by the museum to work on the Star-Spangled Banner. She and her team of workers stitched a linen backing to the flag using a fishnet pattern. The flag soon had twelve to fourteen stitches per square inch for a total of nearly two million stitches.

There was nothing inherently wrong with the approach Fowler took. In fact, the stitches helped hold the flag together all those years so groups of schoolchildren on field trips could admire it hanging on the museum wall. However, the linen backing meant only one side of the flag could be seen.

The current conservators are removing that linen backing in a slow process, snipping free all two million stitches by hand. I mentioned to Thomassen-Krauss that this seemed like grueling work. "All conservation work can be considered painstaking and tedious," she said.

I asked what it felt like to work on such an historic flag. Was there any sense of awe? "I think as you're working you are too busy concentrating," she said. "You don't really have the time or the leisure to think about it too much. You have a job to do."

She pointed out that while the flag is one of the most significant artifacts in the Smithsonian's collection, it is surrounded by items of great historical value, including the lunch counter from the Greensborough, North Carolina, civil rights protest, the desk where Thomas Jefferson wrote the

Declaration of Independence, even the chairs in which Robert E. Lee and Ulysses S. Grant sat as they signed the Confederate surrender that ended the Civil War at Appomattox, Virginia. "You could name thousands of important artifacts," Thomassen-Krauss said.

While Thomassen-Krauss managed to keep a professional detachment from the flag, that was not the case with Officer Green. She had learned everything she could about the flag and shared that knowledge with visitors. "If someone has questions, I want to know the answers," she said.

She has even gone behind the scenes to see what the conservators were up to. They call her Officer Flag Girl and she calls them The Flagettes. "You know, like a musical group," she explained.

She said there is a constant stream of visitors to see the flag. For some, the Star-Spangled Banner sets off a flood of emotions. Some feel compelled to put their hands over their hearts. Some cry. Others sing.

"I had a little girl who was four, she sang the national anthem all the way through," Green said. "I was so impressed. Another time, a boy came through here saying, 'This is so boring.' I said, 'What are you talking about, it's boring? This flag is part of your history, your family's history, your country's history.' So I challenged him. We played a flag quiz game and he left here learning something."

An exhibit tells the story of the flag and the battle of Baltimore. The kid-friendly display had pieces of wool bunting and even shrapnel to touch. Young visitors were eager to show off their newfound knowledge.

"How much does it weigh, mom?" asked a girl.

"Two hundred pounds?"

"Way wrong!" the girl shouted with delight, one up on mom. "Forty-five pounds!"

Upon seeing the exhibit, visitors are sometimes taken

aback by the idea of nineteenth century Americans heartily cutting away pieces of the flag as tokens and souvenirs. Officer Green offers them an explanation. "When you went to the Armisteads' house for dinner, instead of a slice of apple pie for dessert you got a piece of the flag. If you were a really important visitor, you got a star."

Sharing pieces of the flag seemed like a nice tradition to me, considering it was done to honor veterans or simply as a way to connect with history. According to Thomassen-Krauss, the Smithsonian tried to track down all the missing pieces of the flag. Thirteen fragments turned up and were given to the Smithsonian. Finding all the pieces proved impossible. "They were scattered far and wide," she said.

As I left the exhibit, Officer Flag Girl was already busy greeting another group of visitors. "There it is," she proudly announced. "The Star-Spangled Banner."

Thomassen-Krauss pointed out that in creating the flag, Congress had simply declared that it would have stars and stripes, with a red, white and blue color scheme. No symbolic value was placed on the flag. "All of the symbolism has been applied as a result of the culture and history of the flag," she said.

During my visit to Washington, D.C., I was reminded that the flag and the United States are a work in progress. As it happened, I arrived along with 200,000 people who had come to protest President George W. Bush's intent to go to war with Iraq. Our train was jammed with protesters. On the metro platform at the national mall, where we all got out and crept in one human mass toward the exit, I found myself shuffling along next to a man dressed as Uncle Sam, another legacy of the War of 1812.

"So, you're protesting the war," I pointed out with an amazing grasp of the obvious, considering he was holding a large picket sign that stated, *Forget the toys boys! Give diplomacy a chance.*

"Yes," he said warily.

"How about that." The truth was, I didn't know who was right about the looming war. Citizens must have felt the same way leading up to the War of 1812.

At the Smithsonian, on the way to The Star-Spangled Banner exhibit, I passed a huge garrison flag that had hung off the walls of the Pentagon following the September 11, 2001 attack. Visitors clustered beneath, looking up at the Pentagon flag spotted with grease and soot, serving as a reminder that new symbols are being born all the time.

While the Star-Spangled Banner is America's most famous flag, several others are almost as well-known: the Revolutionary War flag with its circle of thirteen stars in a blue field; Old Glory—a generic nickname for all flags—actually comes from the legend of a particular Civil War flag; the Confederate flag remains a lightning rod for political controversy; the most famous flag of the twentieth century was raised by three Marines at the battle of Iwo Jima during World War II.

The current preservation effort at the Smithsonian is meant to ensure the survival of the flag for another 500 years. As Thomassen-Krauss pointed out, in centuries to come the Star-Spangled Banner might inspire new democracies and generations yet unborn. One strand at a time, that preservation effort continues. In the end, it turns out the real enemy of the Star-Spangled Banner was not so much the British, but time itself.

10

Slavery
African-Americans caught in middle of the conflict

1812 was not a war about slavery, unless you happened to be a slave. For many enslaved Americans, the war meant taking sides. Some slaves and free blacks fought for the United States, while others joined the British in hopes that they might win their freedom.

History has painted a clear picture of what the two sides stood for during the War of 1812. Americans defended freedom and democracy while the British represented oppression at the hands of a monarch. Look a little harder at the picture, however, and the edges begin to blur. Was the United States' invasion of Canada an act of liberation or conquest? Freedom applied only to white Americans. Many of the military and government leaders of the United States possessed slaves. President James Madison owned as many as one hundred slaves. The British had outlawed slavery years before. Britain was fighting to overthrow the despot Napoleon and liberate Europe.

Which side was better? Which side was in the right? For slaves and free blacks, it was something of a toss-up. Some were content with the status quo, if not happy about it. It must have been hard for African-Americans to see how the War of 1812 was going to help the cause of freedom. Some free blacks took up muskets and fought courageously in the army or served as sailors in the United States Navy. Other slaves perceived going over to the British as an opportunity for freedom and they took advantage of it. A similar situation had developed during the Revolutionary War, when large numbers of slaves in the South attached themselves to the British army, hoping for freedom. At the end of the Revolution, British promises to help the runaways were empty. They had used the slaves as political pawns just as surely as their American masters used them as cheap labor.

After the War of 1812, the British transported as many as 3,000 former Chesapeake Bay region slaves to Nova Scotia. What a change Nova Scotia's climate must have been for African-Americans used to the Chesapeake region's steamy summer heat and relatively warm winters. The settlers tried to grow crops in the poor soil. In 1821, ninty-five blacks from the Hammond Plains community in Nova Scotia moved on to settle in Trinidad in the West Indies. Today, blacks make up about five percent of the population in Nova Scotia.

Britain abolished the slave trade in 1807, though human bondage as it was practiced in the United States had not existed in England itself since pre-Christian times. The U.S. abolished the slave trade in 1808, making the importation of slaves from Africa illegal. Slavery itself had not been outlawed. The institution of slavery was only just gearing up. Agriculture in the South had not yet exploded into the "King Cotton" economy that would fuel the Civil War of the 1860s. With the need for slaves to work southern cotton plantations, the trade in enslaved humans would burgeon following 1812, no matter what the law said. European nations patrolled the coast of Africa to thwart slavers, but the United States never made any real effort to halt the slave trade. It is estimated that 250,000 more slaves were illegally imported into the United States from 1808 to 1860.

The nation's founders had wrestled with the problem of

slavery but found no easy solutions. In his book *Founding Brothers: The Revolutionary Generation*, Joseph J. Ellis describes the political wrangling that had gone into avoiding a solution to the problem of slavery. As Ellis explains, slavery was a difficult issue even for the Founding Fathers. Ending slavery might also have brought about an end to the young United States as slave-holding states broke away. The agricultural-based Southern economy, including the Virginia plantations of George Washington, Thomas Jefferson and James Madison, depended on slave labor. Even a government-funded gradual emancipation was out of the question. By the end of the Revolution, there was such a huge population of African-Americans that paying to free them would have bankrupted the new nation.

In 1800, the population of the United States included 893,692 slaves. Only a relative few, 36,505, lived north of Maryland. By the time of the 1860 census, there would be nearly four million slaves, most of them living in what would become the Confederate States of America. In some southern states, the population of slaves nearly outnumbered the whites.

With so many enslaved Americans, the threat of an insurrection always bubbled just beneath the surface of Southern life. More than one plantation owner worried about the field hands rising up with knives and axes. The British did not discourage these fears in 1812.

The battle of Caulk's Field in rural Kent County, Maryland, offers an example of how people of color were sometimes caught between the British and Americans during the War of 1812. At Caulk's Field, one slave saw the British as his salvation while a free black man in the King's service was only too glad to flee the Royal Navy.

Leading up to the battle, the Royal Navy carried out a

series of diversionary raids along the Chesapeake Bay to keep American reinforcements occupied while the main British force seized the nation's capital. British raiders struck waterfront farms and towns. During one such raid at the plantation of a family named Frisby, the British liberated four slaves. Considering the value of a slave, the loss to the plantation must have been severe.

One of the slaves offered to guide the British during a nighttime sneak attack against the American militia that had turned out to confront the raiders. The British frequently depended on local slaves to serve as guides, with mixed results. Sometimes, the slaves were loyal to the Americans and intentionally led the British astray. On that summer night nearly two centuries ago, the recently freed slave from the Frisby plantation led the British across the dark woods and fields. When the two forces finally met on a moonlit battlefield, it proved to be a devastating loss for the British, whose commander was killed.

The slave was captured the next day by the Americans, who were intent on hanging him as a traitor. He managed to escape by paddling a canoe out to the British frigate *HMS Menelaus* riding at anchor in the bay. His fate with the British is not known, but it is likely the slave made a new life for himself as a free man. This unnamed slave was willing to lead enemy troops to destroy the only home he had known. It was not just a bid for freedom he was making, but possibly an attempt at revenge.

The Royal Navy also had a man go over to the other side. According to Stan Quick, a local historian who has made an extensive study of Caulk's Field, a black warrant officer deserted on the eve of the battle. Quick speculated that the British sailor probably hid from the British and Americans by mixing in with a free black community near the battlefield. Quick later found the man's name in a census of free blacks living in Montgomery County, Maryland.

The War of 1812 is rife with similar ironies concerning slavery. Across the bay from Caulk's Field, the battle of Baltimore would come to epitomize the fight for freedom. Barely a year after the war ended, the city was becoming a key hub in the slave trade. According to an article by Ralph Clayton published in *The (Baltimore) Sun*, between 1815 and 1860 slave traders made Baltimore one of the leading ports for ships carrying slaves to the deep South. The city was ideally located in a region more interested in selling off its slaves than in importing new ones for labor. Human stockyards sprang up around the harbor. Clayton writes that most of the major slave traders in Baltimore came from Kentucky, Georgia, Virginia and Tennessee.

These slave pens were located along Pratt Street in what is today a busy tourist area between Baltimore's Inner Harbor and Oriole Park at Camden Yards. They were also within a stone's throw of Fort McHenry, where free blacks fought to defend the country that kept fellow members of their race enslaved. The British "invaders" might have sacked and burned the city, but they would have recognized the slaves' right to be free. Although the British were not fighting to free slaves, emancipation would have been a happy consequence if they had won the fight in Baltimore.

In an essay published by *The Sun* in August 2001, Clayton describes the brutal practice of selling slaves.

During the late autumn of 1816, 'a Negro girl, about 17 years of age' was being offered for sale. She was said to be sold for 'no fault' and could be seen by applying at stall No. 2, Center Market.

Several days later, a 'Negro woman, 25 years of age' was auctioned by Charles R. Green at the Horse Market . . . where he advertised 'One may also bid on a number of very fine horses.'

A grim business, indeed.

The British discussed the employment of runaway slaves as part of their military strategy. In his book *Terror on the Chesapeake*, historian Christopher T. George relates a plan proposed by British Lieutenant Colonel Charles Napier that would make use of runaways to bring a swift end to the war.

Napier wrote in his memoirs,

Seeing a black population of slaves ruled by a thin population of whites, the blacks thinking the English demi-gods (for liberating them) and their Yankee masters devils, I said to the authorities, "Give me two hundred thousand stand of arms, and land me in Virginia with only the officers and non-commissioned officers of three black regiments, that is to say about one hundred persons accustomed to drill black men. . . The multitude of blacks who nightly come to our ships, and whom we drive back to death or renewed slavery, shows that we can in a week assemble a million – certainly one hundred thousand before any force could reach us . . . All the blacks can use arms, and in twelve hours can be organized in regiments and brigades. . . When this vast mass shall be collected and armed, we shall roll down the coast, and our large fleet can pass us into the Delaware country, out of which we shall instantly chase the whole population. Then, with half our fleet in the Delaware River, with provisions in the Delaware country, and a handful of corn or rice is all a black slave will want for that occasion, we shall people the deserted space, set all the women and children to cultivate the ground, and with our enormous mass of males, will have entrenched a position across the isthmus (between the Delaware and Chesapeake bays) in twenty-four hours...

Napier then goes on to claim how he would have captured Washington while British forces swooped down from Canada to the end of the war. In hindsight, it sounds like the sort of plan hatched over one too many glasses of port, but Napier's enthusiasm does show that the British encountered many runaway slaves who were willing to fight for their freedom. Surely, their hopes must have been dashed by Britain's defeat and withdrawal.

British leaders did make an attempt to use former slaves as soldiers, in part to encourage more runaways and thus deny mid-Atlantic plantations of their labor force. Nothing as dramatic as Napier's plan came about. Vice Admiral Sir Alexander Cochrane issued a proclamation intended for the ears of slaves:

(you) will have (the) choice of either entering into His Majesty's sea or land forces, or of being sent as free settlers to the British possessions in North America or the West Indies, where (you) will meet with all due encouragement.

Admiral Cockburn went so far as to train Colonial Marines on Tangier Island in the Chesapeake Bay. These former slaves were paid a bounty of twenty dollars, given muskets and fancy red uniforms, and drilled as marines. The troops eventually saw action in shore raids on Virginia. Cockburn later praised this unit for "the Conduct of . . . the Colonial Marines, who were for the first time, employed in Arms against their old Masters, and behaved to the admiration of every Body."

While runaway slaves often sought refuge with the British,

free blacks sometimes came to the defense of the very country that had kept them enslaved. Some served in American ships or in special "colored" units, such as the 26th U.S. Infantry Regiment, made up of recruits from Philadelphia. Free blacks fought at the battle of Lake Erie and most notably at New Orleans.

No matter how hard African-Americans fought for either side, it was impossible to overcome society's prejudices against them. A reminder of this comes from none other than James Madison. The Father of the Constitution was troubled by slavery, but not enough to be a reformer. While he was described as a "good master," he did not set his slaves free. Madison's commitment to a free democracy while relying on slave labor at his Virginia plantation seems hard to reconcile today.

A "Q&A" with James Madison from 1823 offers some insights into what he thought about the institution of slavery and the character of African-Americans. The brevity of some responses is maddening for anyone who wants to know more about his views on slavery.

At the time, Madison was no longer president but living in retirement at Montpelier. He received a letter from Dr. Jedidiah Morse that contained thirty-four questions regarding slavery. The questions were purportedly from an English abolitionist. Here are some of the more relevant responses as published in the James Madison University magazine:

Hon. James Madison, Esq.
New Haven, Mar. 14, 1823
Sir,
The foregoing was transmitted to me from a respectable correspondent in Liverpool, deeply engaged in the abolition of the slave trade, and the amelioration of the condition of slaves. If, sir, your leisure will allow you,

and it is agreeable to you to furnish brief answers to these questions, you will, I conceive, essentially serve the cause of humanity, and gratify and oblige the Society above named, and Sir, with high consideration and esteem, your most ob't serv't,
JED'H MORSE.

Do the planters generally live on their own estates?
Yes.

Does a planter with ten or fifteen slaves employ an overlooker, or does he overlook his slaves himself?
Employs an overseer for that number of slaves, with few exceptions.

Is it a common or general practice to mortgage slave estates?
Not uncommonly the land; sometimes the slaves; very rarely both together.

Are sales of slave estates very frequent under execution for debt, and what proportion of the whole may be thus sold annually?
The common law, as in England, governs the relation between land and debts; slaves are often sold under execution for debt; the proportion to the whole cannot be great within a year, and varies, of course, with the amount of debts and the urgency of creditors.

Does the Planter possess the power of selling the different branches of a family separate?
Yes.

Is it the general system to employ the Negroes in task

work, or by the day?
Slaves seldom employed in regular task work. They
prefer it only when rewarded with the surplus time
gained by their industry.

Are there many small plantations where the owners
possess only a few slaves? What proportion of the whole
may be supposed to be held in this way?
Very many, and increasing with the progressive
subdivisions of property; the proportion cannot be
stated.

In such cases, are the slaves treated or almost
considered a part of the family?
The fewer the slaves, the fewer the holders of slaves,
the greater the indulgence and familiarity. In districts
composing large masses of slaves there is no difference
in their condition, whether held in small or large
numbers beyond the difference in the dispositions of
the owners, and the greater strictness of attention where
the number is greater.

In what state are the slaves as to religion or religious
instruction?
There is no general system of religious instruction.
There are few spots where religious worship is not
within reach, and to which they do not resort. Many are
regular members of Congregations, chiefly Baptist; and
some Preachers also, though rarely able to read.

Is it common for the slaves to be regularly married?
Not common; but instances are increasing.

If a man forms an attachment to a woman on a different

or distant plantation, is it the general practice for some accommodation to take place between the owners of the man and woman, so that they may live together?

The accommodation not unfrequent where the plantations are very distant. The slaves prefer wives on a different plantation, as affording occasions and pretexts for going abroad, and exempting them on holidays from a share of the little calls to which those at home are liable.

In the United States of America, the slaves are found to increase at about the rate of 3 percent per annum. Does the same take place in other places? Give a census, if such is taken. Show what cause contributes to this increase, or what prevents it where it does not take place.

The remarkable increase of slaves, as shewn by the census, results from the comparative defect of moral and prudential restraint on the sexual connexion; and from the absence, at the same, of that counteracting licentiousness of intercourse, of which the worst examples are to be traced where the African trade, as in the West Indies, kept the number of females less than of the males.

Obtain a variety of estimates from the Planters of the cost of bringing up a child, and at what age it becomes a clear gain to its owner.

The annual expense of food and raiment in rearing a child may be stated at about 8, 9, or 10 dollars; and the age at which it begins to be gainful to its owner about 9 or 10 years.

Obtain information respecting the comparative

cheapness of cultivation by slaves or by free men.
The practice here does not furnish data for a comparison of cheapness between these two modes of cultivation.

Is it common for the free blacks to labour in the field?
They are sometimes hired for field labour in time of time of harvest, and on other particular occasions.

Where the labourers consist of free blacks and of white men, what are the relative prices of their labour when employed about the same work?
The examples are too few to have established any such relative prices.

Is it considered that the increase in the proportion of free blacks to slaves increases or diminishes the danger of insurrection?
Rather increases.

Are the free blacks employed in the defence of the Country, and do they and the Creoles preclude the necessity of European troops?
(No answer)

Do the free blacks appear to consider themselves as more closely connected with the slaves or with the white population? and in cases of insurrection, with which have they generally taken part?
More closely with the slaves, and more likely to side with them in a case of insurrection.

What is their general character with respect to industry and order, as compared with that of the slaves?

Generally idle and depraved; appearing to retain the bad qualities of the slaves, with whom they continue to associate, without acquiring any of the good ones of the whites, from whom [they] continue separated by prejudices against their colour, and other peculiarities.

Are there any instances of emancipation in particular estates, and what is the result?
There are occasional instances in the present legal condition of leaving the State.

Is there any general plan of emancipation in progress, and what?
None.

What was the mode and progress of emancipation in those States in America where slavery has ceased to exist?
(No answer)

What about slavery from the perspective of a slave? For that, we have the reminiscences of Paul Jennings, a slave owned by James and Dolley Madison. Jennings was born at the Madison family's Montpelier estate in 1799 and became a body servant to Madison. Long after the War of 1812, Dolley sold him for $120 to the prominent Massachusetts politician, Daniel Webster. He granted Jennings his freedom but made him work off the debt at the rate of $8 per month.

Jennings, articulate and literate, was also half white. Considering he had to buy his freedom, Jennings has relatively good things to say about the Madisons. Many years later, when the elderly Dolley Madison was destitute, he often brought her food and small necessities.

Jennings wrote,

While I was a servant to Mr. Webster, he often sent me
to her (Dolley) with a market-basket full of provisions,
and told me whenever I saw anything in the house that
I thought she was in need of, to take it to her. I often did
this, and occasionally gave her small sums from my own
pocket, though I had years before bought my freedom
of her.

Mr. Madison, I think, was one of the best men that
ever lived. I never saw him in a passion, and never knew
him to strike a slave, although he had over one hundred;
neither would he allow an overseer to do it. Whenever
any slaves were reported to him stealing or 'cutting up'
badly, he would send for them and admonish them
privately, and never mortify them by doing it before
others. They generally served him faithfully.

Throughout the War of 1812, the issue of slavery
remained in the background. Even as the new nation spread
westward and prospered, the geographic boundaries between
north and south, slave state and free state, had been drawn.
Confrontations over slavery would fester for the next few
decades.

Slavery would not be abolished in the United States until
January 1, 1863, when President Abraham Lincoln issued the
emancipation proclamation. Slaves in Kentucky, Missouri,
Maryland and Delaware were not set free at that time because
Lincoln was concerned about the political ramifications in
these critical border states. Slavery continued in Delaware
and Kentucky until December 1865, eight months after the
end of the Civil War, making the United States one of the last
western nations to outlaw the practice. By the time the
thirteenth Amendment to James Madison's Constitution was
ratified, as many as twenty-four million African men, women

and children had been carried aboard slave ships to North and South America and the Caribbean.

The seeds of change had been planted in 1812. It would take a bloody civil war to settle the matter once and for all, bringing a painful end to an issue the Founding Fathers had done their best to avoid.

Photo by David Healey

Montpelier, the Virginia plantation home of President James Madison.

The house in Brookeville, Md., that became temporary headquarters for the United States government in exile.

Photo by David Healey

Two cannonballs dug from the ground at Elk Landing on display at the Hollingsworth House. They were probably left over from the skirmish with British troops.

Photo by David Healey

Photo by David Healey

National Park Ranger Scott Sheads leads a "flag talk" at Fort McHenry while visitors unfurl a full-size replica of the Star Spangled Banner.

Photo by David Healey

The Caulk's Field monument in Kent County, Md., marks the battlefield where Captain Sir Peter Parker and 14 other British troops died.

Photo by Adelma Gregory Bunnell

Concord Point Light stands near where John O'Neill mounted his single-handed defense of Havre de Grace when the British attacked in May 1813.

Courtesy The Star Spangled Banner Flag House

Mary Young Pickersgill, seated at right, works on the Star Spangled
Banner as Fort McHenry Commander George Armistead and
Commodore Joshua Barney, at left, look on. At right is Gen. John Stricker.

Courtesy The Star Spangled Banner Flag House

Photo by David Healey

Days after the terrorist attack on
Sept. 11, 2001, the Fort McHenry
flag flies at half-mast.

Mary Young Pickersgill was an
enterprising Baltimore flag maker
and socially conscious
businesswoman.

11

James Madison
In search of a Founding Father at his Virginia plantation

A hot wind blew across the Virginia fields at Montpelier, bending the grass and revealing the white bellies of leaves in the treetops. This was James Madison's home, a 2,600-acre plantation once worked by scores of slaves.

Remote and little-changed in 200 years, Montpelier seemed like a good place to try to understand Madison, who remains something of an enigma to twenty-first century Americans. Some of his spirit must surely linger here.

The earliest known painting of Madison, made when he was about thirty-five years old, shows a pale, baby-faced man—far different from the fierce old visage of later portraits. Powdered wigs of colonial times gave way to unruly white hair, like a lion's mane. His face, as we know him best, is thin and fox-like, especially as he grows older. The brown eyes are daunting. They stare from the canvas, appraising you. He could pass for a shrewd old banker. James Madison was nobody's fool.

Born at Montpelier in 1751 to a long-established Virginia family, Madison was a child of wealth and privilege. Generations earlier, Madisons had carved their farm out of the Virginia frontier. One of James Madison's distant uncles was slain fighting Indians.

Small and bookish, Madison was an unlikely leader, even

though he was born into Virginia's elite. He took up his studies at an early age and could read several languages, including Greek. He had a library of more than 4,000 books at a time when the average family owned only a Bible.

He studied at the College of New Jersey, at what would become known as Princeton. By his twenties he became a leader in the revolution. The fact that Madison was the lone delegate to take notes at the Constitutional Convention in 1787 shows not only that he understood the importance of what was taking place, but also his scholarly nature. His notes provide the only record of events.

Despite his wealth and intellect, Madison did not present a striking figure. His friends called him "Jemmy." He was prematurely balding and just five-feet, four-inches tall. The other Founding Fathers literally towered over him. George Washington was six-feet, two-inches tall and Jefferson was six-feet, two and one-half inches.

Madison habitually wore black. His style of dress, monkish and modest, was old-fashioned by 1812. He insisted on breeches and hose, and shoes with buckles, when full-length trousers were becoming the standard for men.

Observers of the day described Madison as witty, warm and entertaining in small groups or at dinner. Yet he adopted a stiff and wooden public persona, which he considered appropriately dignified for a president.

Madison was a determined politician, apparently employing what we might call today a passive aggressive personality. In his book *Founding Brothers: The Revolutionary Generation*, Joseph J. Ellis describes Madison as the master of the inoffensive argument in his career as a legislator. It was impossible to get mad at him without seeming unreasonable because he was so mild and polite. "He seemed to lack a personal agenda because he seemed to lack a personality," Ellis writes. "Yet when the votes were counted, his side always won." As one observer of the day put it, "Never have I seen so *much* mind in so *little* matter."

Some historians speculate that Madison never would have become president if it had not been for his wife, Dolley. Wherever she went, she cast a glow. She could dazzle an individual or a crowd. Before becoming first lady, she had served as White House hostess throughout the presidential term of Thomas Jefferson. When Madison took office in 1808, the White House had eighteen staff members to do the cooking, carry messages and perform other duties at the executive mansion. By 1989, the Reagan White House would employ 3,366 staff members.

Louisa Catherine Adams, wife of John Quincy Adams, offered this recollection of the president and first lady that leaves little doubt as to who wore the pants—or breeches—in the White House.

> Mr. Madison was a very small man in his person, with a very large head—his manners were peculiarly unassuming; and his conversation lively, often playful ... His language was chaste, well-suited to occasion ...
>
> Mrs. Madison was tall, large and rather masculine in personal dimensions; her complexion was so fair and brilliant as to redeem this objection, in its perfectly feminine beauty . . . There was a frankness and ease in her deportment, that won golden opinions from all, and she possessed an influence so decided with her little Man.

Madison was a master legislator, but he was ill-suited to the leadership role required of a president. To this unassuming chief executive fell the task of guiding the young United States through its second war of revolution.

"Madison made some very bad appointments of generals at

the outbreak of the war," said Devin Bent, retired director of the James Madison Center at James Madison University. "But Madison later made some very good appointments—William Henry Harrison in the northwest and Andrew Jackson in the southeast."

Bent points to the defeat of the British and Tecumseh at the battle of the Thames, an event immortalized in a painting at the Capitol dome. Then there was the defeat of the Creek Indian confederation by Andrew Jackson at the battle of Horseshoe Bend. Bent notes that both Harrison and Jackson were later elected president.

"We might think of two stages of the war—the first half in which the British were vulnerable since they were engaged in fighting Napoleon in Europe—this portion of the war was bungled by the United States," Bent says. "However, even in this portion of the war there were significant victories by the United States." The second stage of the war would come after the defeat of Napoleon, when the British began pouring resources into the American war.

When it comes to naming America's greatest presidents, most historians don't include Madison. Historian Garry Wills has written that Madison does not make it to the Top Ten list of presidents on account of unfortunate circumstances, a temperament that better suited a legislator than a leader, and several errors in misreading the intentions of Britain. "One could say that Madison was just dealt a bad hand," Wills writes in his history of the Madison presidency.

According to the *Getty Thesaurus of Geographical Names*, there are 196 locations in the United States named after James Madison. These include several towns, bays in Louisiana and Maryland, fourteen creeks, three good-sized cities, a Madison Butte and Madison Beach, and at least twenty counties and parishes. While "Washington" remains the most popular place name in America—with thirty-two Washington counties, for starters—nineteenth century Americans clearly did not see the fourth president as a failure.

"Madison went out as a hero," said Rich Kall, resident War of 1812 expert at Montpelier. "He got all the credit for winning the war. Twice, we beat the most powerful nation on Earth, and that was no accident."

The previous day, we had visited Monticello, home of Madison's good friend and collaborator, Thomas Jefferson. Monticello was evocative and inspiring, but it was crowded. In comparison, Montpelier was nearly deserted. If it had been for sale, the mansion itself might have been described as "needing work."

Far off the beaten path, Montpelier was free of any noise from passing traffic or planes. The only sound was the breeze rushing over the fields. I was beginning to notice how many historical sites related to the War of 1812 were such peaceful locations.

The mansion is an interesting shade of pink. When you first come up the long drive and get a glimpse of the house, the sheer size of it takes your breath away. There are seventy rooms. Most were added by William duPont after he bought the house in 1900. When it was James Madison's house there were just eleven rooms, but it was grand enough for the day.

Inside, Montpelier was a restoration work in progress. Patches of old wallpaper had been peeled away to reveal the bare plaster walls. Furniture from the Madison era was scattered throughout the rooms. Oriental carpets covered unfinished floors. The windows lacked curtains.

Historical architects had been cutting more than 200 holes in the walls, some of which you could still see, poking and prodding to find out what the house looked like in Madison's time. Tour guide Marianne Ashurst said that Montpelier had just undergone the most intensive study of historical architecture of any house in America. Among the items that turned up were nails made at Jefferson's nailery at Monticello.

The day we visited, architects and historians were on the back terrace, studying plans and deciding where all the authenticated furniture would go. The end result would be a beautifully restored mansion, but we found it more enjoyable to see Montpelier while it felt like somebody's neglected house rather than a museum.

Many occupants besides the Madisons had left their stamp on Montpelier. After nine years of crop losses forced Dolley to auction the estate, six different families lived in the mansion. Then, in 1900, the duPont family arrived. One of their children, Marion duPont Scott, lived in the house all her life. At her death in 1983 at age ninety-two, she left the home and grounds to the National Trust. Since then, there has been a slow return to the Madison era at Montpelier.

According to Ashurst, the Madisons' original furniture was sold off as part of the sheriff's auction Dolley was forced to hold. "Some of it we've been given back, some of it we're still begging for," Ashurst said. "We have a long, long wish list."

Two of the pieces that have been authenticated are the Madisons' canopied bed, visible in an unrestored upstairs room, and a small pine daybed that Dolley had carried into her husband's study in his later years when he was bedridden there, so that the long-married couple could spend their nights in the same room. "I think it's really a story that tells of great devotion on Dolley's part," Ashurst said.

The duPonts turned Dolley's elegant bedroom into a kitchen, complete with dingy linoleum and a cast-iron sink. Madison's study was gone, long since turned into a hallway during a duPont-era expansion. "You have to remember that people were less aware of historical significance than we are today," Ashurst said. "This was their house, not a museum, and they were free to do with it whatever they wanted."

Madison died in his study on June 28, 1836, ending a strange presidential phenomenon. Years before, Jefferson, John Adams and James Monroe had all died on the Fourth of July. Jefferson and Adams died on the same July Fourth in 1826, just hours apart. Monroe died on July 4, 1831. If Madison had held on just a few days more, he might have made future presidents very nervous.

"Maybe he saved future presidents from going through that sort of ritual and dreading the Fourth of July," Ashurst said. "James Madison died on a day of his own choosing."

For such a frail man who was described as always being on the verge of some fatal illness, Madison had managed to live to age eighty-five, outlasting all the other members of the Revolutionary generation. "Having outlived so many of my contemporaries," Madison once said, "I ought not to forget that I may be thought to have outlived myself."

The nearest you can come today to meeting James Madison is in the person of John Douglas Hall, who makes his living as an historical performer portraying the fourth president. "I've taken my life and reversed it two hundred years," explained Hall, who bears an amazing resemblance to the wiry Founding Father. He is the same height as Madison, and his long white hair adds to the historical impression.

Hall's age in the twenty-first century matches what Madison's would have been that same day two centuries before. When I interviewed hall on September 5, 2001, he explained that for him it was September 5, 1801. Madison's presidency and the War of 1812 had not yet happened.

Hall undertakes his portrayal by being as studious as Madison. First on his daily reading list are the various newspapers of the day, including the *Alexandria Gazette*, *Maryland Gazette* and *National Intelligencer*, that the fourth president would have read.

"I read gazettes as they come in," he said. "This allows me to keep everything in perspective. "I don't read ahead. It's just easier for me to cope with life as I'm leading it. It's allowed me a lot more legitimacy."

He pores over Madison's correspondence and writings by the president's contemporaries. He copies out by hand Madison's personal notes on various topics. The re-writing gives him a perspective on what Madison was actually thinking. This helps him, too, in trying to project the impressions Madison formed of the people around him. Hall tries to read between the lines to discover what Madison really thought. All that background material proves useful. He said he may not use it for months, but then it comes to mind and becomes part of his Madison persona.

Hall has been portraying Madison since 1986. Many nights of the week, you will also find him at Gadsby's Tavern, an eighteenth century establishment in Old Town Alexandria, Virginia. There, he performs period tavern music and shares anecdotes about colonial life in Alexandria. Reluctantly, he stopped being Madison to talk about himself.

"I try to keep John Hall out of the whole thing," he said. "I have so much respect for James Madison that I don't want to water him down with John Douglas Hall."

Hall is part of a trend in taking the portrayal of living history very seriously. You won't see him on TV commercials in a fake wig hawking mattresses for a Presidents' Day sale. The real-life James Madison would have considered that vulgar. You won't find him chatting on a cell phone or working on a computer, either.

"It's a constant struggle to maintain your sense of integrity for what you're doing," he said. "That sense of integrity is so important."

Hall has taken part in anniversary celebrations at James Madison University and in the unveiling of a new postal stamp honoring Madison. When speaking in public as Madison, he prefers a dignified setting. It's better if the lights are dim to diminish distractions to the eye and mimic colonial-era candlelight. He wants the audience to focus on James Madison.

"I don't consider it a theatrical production at all," Hall explained. "I want to make it as easy as possible for people to actually meet James Madison. If they ever had a chance to meet him, this is their opportunity. We live our lives and we are who we are. That's how I try to portray Madison."

To make his point about what he is trying to accomplish in his portrayal, Hall used an example of how 1812 re-enactors at Fort Washington on the nearby Potomac River might act. "If you ask a soldier a question and he answers, 'Well, the soldiers would have done this or would have done that,' it falls short of saying, 'I do this and we do that.' It's the difference between being a guide and actually portraying history," he said. "Some portrayals are based on greater integrity than others. The better ones set a precedent. In fact, there are a lot of good portrayals out there."

Newspapers and correspondence create a written record of Madison's life, but Hall can only guess at private conversations between the president and those around him. One of Madison's most intriguing friendships was with Thomas Jefferson. They also made an effective political team, the Dynamic Duo of eighteenth century politics, with Madison as the junior member. Hall tries to imagine what the two might have discussed at dinner as the candles burned down and they lingered over glasses of red Madeira wine.

Hall said the War of 1812 was mainly about American jurisprudence versus British common law, but the larger question being settled regarded the destiny of the United States as an independent nation or one that was subservient to European powers. The War of 1812 put the idealism of the young United States to its first real test. What was the stuff of which these former colonials and loose-knit states were made? The Constitution, authored largely by Madison, had never withstood such a crisis. Would this document ensuring basic rights and civil liberties survive or would the realities and turmoil of war sweep American idealism aside?

For Hall, the question Madison faced in 1812 boils down to this, "Which way were we Americans going to go?"

12

The Star-Spangled Banner
The story of the national anthem

A fifth-grade class at Daly Elementary School in Elkhart, Indiana, made the national news in September 2002 when the students rewrote the lyrics of the national anthem as a class exercise. "We changed the words so a younger child could understand," teacher Adriana Burton was reported as saying. "They were reading the lyrics and said, 'Gosh, what does this mean?'"

In an attempt to modernize the song, students broke out their thinking caps and a thesaurus. It was also a way to help explain the meaning of the original words to the children. The words "rampart" and "parapet" became "walls." Stripes were not "broad" but "wide." The words "perilous" and "gallantly" became "dangerous" and "bravely."

As reported in the *South Bend Tribune* and *Elkhart Truth* newspapers, the goal was to rewrite the poem/song with comprehension in mind, not rhythm or rhyme. The *Elkhart Truth* noted, "Burton said she knew the assignment had been successful when one of her students spotted a child on the playground wall and said, 'Hey, Mrs. Burton, he's on the rampart!'"

Some critics would like to see *The Star-Spangled Banner* lose its status as national anthem, replaced by a song that is easier to sing. There are several contenders for a new anthem, such as *God Bless America* or even *My Country 'Tis of Thee.* The song that seems best-positioned to replace the national anthem is *America the Beautiful* because of its appealing simplicity.

When asked if the song written by Francis Scott Key would ever be replaced by *America the Beautiful* or another contender, Sarah Scanlan, associate director for public relations and marketing at the Maryland Historical Society, said she had her doubts. Francis Scott Key's handwritten original poem is kept on display at the society in Baltimore.

"For now, I think *The Star-Spangled Banner* is still that rallying song. *God Bless America* is a beautiful song, for example, but if you want people to get up and go patriotically, *The Star-Spangled Banner* is still the best choice. The message is that freedom does not come cheaply. You have to be ready to defend it. "This poem expresses all of our patriotic feelings," she said. "It just has that upbeat, marching, get-up-and-go tune. I think the song has withstood the test of time for all these reasons."

Of all the stories passed down from the War of 1812, the one that Americans know best is how Francis Scott Key came to write the poem that would become the national anthem. In a flash of inspiration, Key jotted the poem on the back of an envelope as he watched the bombardment of Fort McHenry. In that moment, America's most patriotic song was born, although Congress did not adopt *The Star-Spangled Banner* as the national anthem until 1931.

Key was born in 1780 at Terra Rubra Farm near Keymar in Carroll County, Maryland. The farm's Latin name translates to "red earth," soil that is still farmed today. The 149-acre farm, along with Key's house, has changed ownership twice since 2002 after being occupied previously by the same family for twenty-nine years. There is a small, marble monument to Key on the farm and a United States flag flies high above the fields. The farm is not open to the public, but that does not stop curious amateur historians from knocking on the door about once a month. They are disappointed to learn that a wind storm in 1858 destroyed the original house.

Key studied law, and by his early thirties, was a respected lawyer in the Washington suburb of Georgetown, where he lived with his wife and eleven children. He also served as an officer in the local militia.

In his spare time, Key wrote poetry. When he witnessed the battle of Baltimore, it was only natural that he would be inspired to write about the event. None of his other poems have endured, but grateful Marylanders have named schools, highways, bridges, a shopping mall and even a minor league baseball team after the author of *The Star-Spangled Banner.*

The young lawyer witnessed the battle while on a diplomatic mission. He was in Baltimore to accompany John Steuart Skinner, the United States' agent for the release of prisoners of war, to intervene on behalf of a Maryland physician, Dr. William Beanes.

Dr. Beanes lived in Upper Marlboro at the time of the British attack on Washington. Twenty years before, he had emigrated from Scotland. Beanes, an outspoken opponent of the war, was one of the few residents of his small town to stay behind when the British invaded. He willingly offered supplies to the Redcoats, who bought horses and other goods from him. He even gave at least one officer a free supply of tea, sugar and milk.

When a group of thieving British stragglers appeared in town, Beanes and some neighbors captured them. British commander General Robert Ross became irate when he heard that Beanes was interfering with his troops. The general believed that the doctor's earlier hospitality now seemed insincere.

Ross dealt harshly with the doctor. The sixty-five-year-old Beanes was arrested and imprisoned aboard the *HMS Tonnant* under the worst conditions, not even being allowed a change of clothing during two weeks of captivity. Beanes was accused of being a traitor to the crown by reason of his Scottish roots. The punishment for traitors was hanging. Never mind that he was a naturalized United States citizen.

Key, who was a friend of Beanes, was asked by one of the doctor's patients to help obtain his release. It was Skinner who was acting in an official capacity. Skinner was carrying several letters written on Beanes' behalf by wounded British soldiers, praising the doctor for treating them. Historians speculate the letters were why Beanes was spared, rather than any persuasive arguments made by Skinner or Key.

During his stay aboard *Tonnant,* Key developed a low opinion of the British. He dined and conversed with the three top British leaders in the Chesapeake Bay region, Vice Admiral Sir Alexander Cochrane, Rear Admiral Sir George Cockburn and General Ross, who would soon be killed leading his troops in an attempt to capture Baltimore. Key had expected refinement in these British aristocrats. Three weeks after the battle he wrote to a friend,

> Never was a man more disappointed in his expectations than I have been as to the character of British officers. With some exceptions they appeared to be illiberal, ignorant and vulgar, seem filled with a spirit of malignity against everything American.

While Key and Skinner were treated as guests, technically they were prisoners. The British would not let the Americans return to Baltimore for fear that they would give away details of the impending attack. Guarded by British marines, they were allowed to return with Dr. Beanes to their own sloop anchored at the mouth of the Patapsco River. From this prime vantage point, they watched the bombardment of Fort McHenry.

At dawn, as the darkness and mist lifted, Francis Scott Key was thrilled to see the huge United States flag—not the Union Jack—waving above the fort. Key jotted down a few lines of poetry and some notes capturing his feelings at that moment. Over the next few days, still held captive by the British, then later at the Indian Queen Hotel in Baltimore after his release, he reworked those rough beginnings into thirty-two lines of verse, creating a poem made up of four stanzas.

The poem was an immediate sensation. Copies were distributed around Baltimore and among the defenders at Fort McHenry. Key had written the words to match the tune of a popular British drinking song, *To Anacreon in Heaven.* Key's brother-in-law, Judge J.H. Nicholson, was so impressed by the poem that he had handbills made up and distributed under the title *The Defence of Fort M'Henry.* Key's poem was published in the *Baltimore Patriot* newspaper on September 20, 1814, then reprinted in newspapers from New Hampshire to Georgia. In October, an actor gave a public performance of the poem in Baltimore, calling it, *The Star-Spangled Banner.*

Key never sought to profit from his creation. He continued to write poetry and practice law, going on to argue cases before the United States Supreme Court. He died in 1843 at his "red earth" farm.

In the summer of 2002, Francis Scott Key's original copy of the poem at the Maryland Historical Society in Baltimore was spirited away for some long-awaited repairs. The document has since been secured in a new frame filled with argon gas, an improvement over the sealed frame in which the poem was placed in the 1950s. According to the historical society's Sarah Scanlan, the poem returned to public display in November 2003 as part of an exhibit called "Looking for Liberty in Maryland."

Scanlan said that while the historical society is too far removed from the tourist district to attract crowds, visitors make the pilgrimage to see *The Star-Spangled Banner.* She said historical tourism is just like real estate, "It's all about location, location, location."

"Whenever people come to Baltimore, they think of Fort McHenry before they think of the Maryland Historical Society," she said. "Still, people do come in. I've seen whole families in the gallery gather around to read the words and sometimes they even sing them together. They're amazed because there are four verses—and they sing them all. It's very moving."

Those curious about the poem can view it online at various websites, but what you usually see is the handwritten document from the Library of Congress collection. The Baltimore version, also handwritten, is actually an earlier draft and does not bear Key's signature. It also has several cross-outs where Key changed words.

"It looks like a work in progress," Scanlan said. "It's really interesting to see the process involved in writing the poem." One of the conservators at the Maryland Historical Society who has been closely involved in preserving the document is Mary Herbert, associate director for special collections. She explained that the poem was sent to the Conservation Center for Art and Historical Artifacts in Philadelphia, where experts made minor repairs to small tears and a dog-eared corner.

"As with most documents in family hands, it was just folded up and tucked away somewhere," she said, noting that the original was passed down through Key's family. In the early 1950s, the document was encased in a kind of glass "sandwich" filled with helium, so the original poem actually has been in a fairly stable environment for the past fifty years. The conservation work done in Philadelphia should help preserve the document for several more years. There are limitations to how well it can be protected from further deterioration.

Special care will have to be taken when the document is exhibited in years to come. "It has already received its lifetime quota of light," she said, explaining that too much light damages the ink and paper. "We've got to be very careful about the light levels."

As for the future, "We can't always have our national treasures around even though we do the best we can to preserve them," she said. "We shouldn't be selfish and want to see them all the time or they won't be there for the next generation."

Herbert said that while having the original document written by Key is nice, it's really the poem itself—and the national anthem—that have enduring power. "It was a resounding victory showing that this young America was capable of governing and defending itself," she said of the battle of Baltimore. "The battle was extremely important to these Baltimoreans especially because they were the ones under attack. Washington had just been burned and the British had this superior force in terms of numbers and naval supremacy, but with the victory in Baltimore we sent a message that 'You may have gotten us but you didn't get us good.'"

While most Americans are familiar with the first verse, they might be surprised at the warlike tone of the rest of the anthem.

Their blood has wash'd out their foul footsteps' pollution.

No refuge could save the hireling and slave
From the terror of flight or the gloom of the grave . . .

Such venomous language directed at the British feels out
of place in the twenty-first century, when our nation's old
adversary is probably America's closest friend. Then again,
the words could just as easily apply to any enemy of America.
One of the most poignant aspects of the song has nothing to
do with the language, but with punctuation. The song ends in
a question mark. Francis Scott Key is not just asking if Fort
McHenry has survived, but seems to be posing a challenge for
generations of Americans yet to come.

Oh, say does that star-spangled banner yet wave
O'er the land of the free and the home of the brave?

13

Oh, Say Can He Sing!
Singing the national anthem at Baltimore's Camden Yards and beyond

A grand re-opening celebration was taking place at the Wal-Mart. A crowd of sixty staff members in blue nylon vests mingled with a handful of local politicians who looked uncomfortable in their suits on a steamy August morning. The group had gathered in the aisle between the men's and women's clothing departments. Red, white and blue balloons hovered above the racks. It was only 8:00 AM and the smell of brewing coffee wafted through the store.

The store manager started the festivities with a rousing welcome. "Good morning everybody!" Sixty employees responded with one voice, "Good morning! Welcome to Wal-Mart! *Unnghh!*"

In a ceremony that felt like a pep rally wrapped up inside a religious revival, the staff of the Elkton Wal-Mart was celebrating the completion of long weeks of hard work they had spent rearranging the stock, moving departments, shifting whole aisles of merchandise.

They had done well. Shelves of neatly folded clothing formed a colorful background for the event, the white tile floors gleamed with a new coat of wax, and all the staff looked proud. Large white letters on their vests spelled out, *How may I help you?*

If there is any temple of plenty for middle- and working-class Americans, it must be a store such as this, stuffed floor to ceiling with acres of food, clothing, hunting and fishing gear, hardware and house wares. This particular store was even built on the site of a previous local icon, the drive-in movie theatre that closed years ago when VCRs and videotapes took the place of outdoor movies on muggy summer nights.

A preacher led a prayer, checks were handed out to Boy Scout troops and local charities, and there was a lot of clapping as the manager recognized those employees who had worked especially hard to transform the store. One by one, the assistant managers all had something to say, praising their fellow employees. Then Ken, a regional manager who had flown in for the event, got to the bottom line. "Ya'll certainly have reason to be proud," he drawled. "Ya'll never had a decrease during the entire remodel!"

Next came a more solemn moment, the singing of the national anthem. Dressed all in black, local performer Jack Foreaker took position next to the men's belts and without any fanfare or musical accompaniment began to sing.

"O, say can you see . . ."

At the front of the store, cash registers blipped and the electronic doors whisked open and closed. His voice overpowered that background noise as he brought the song to its stirring conclusion. In the appreciative silence that followed, a blue-vested employee whispered, "Wow. I can only sing like that in the shower."

The Star-Spangled Banner is not easy to sing, and nobody knows that better than Foreaker, who, his performance done, was already melting back into the racks of menswear.

Foreaker has earned a local reputation for singing the national anthem. He has been asked to sing the anthem at peach festivals, Little League games and other events, all the result of his moment in the spotlight when he was invited by the Baltimore Orioles to perform at the Camden Yards ballpark.

Foreaker is no stranger to performing in front of crowds. When not working as a counselor, he gives puppet shows that mix Broadway show tunes with a bit of slapstick humor. He has toured with the comedian Gallagher, warming up the crowd with a half-hour act. He has performed with the Beach Boys, Roy Clark, the Oakridge Boys and the cast of *Les Miserables*. He worked off and on with the late Jim Henson and was a puppeteer in some of Henson's Muppet films. Singing the anthem has become his specialty.

"It's an old English song. It's got about ten verses, although most people don't know that because it's hard enough remembering the first one. It's not an easy song to sing because of the range required," he said, noting the mixture of low and high notes. "If you get the first note right, you're okay, but if you don't, you're in trouble. It's that piece in the middle that's the tricky part for me."

He said the difficulty comes from the way a singer's throat contracts to make the sounds. Switching from an "a" sound to an "e" sound, for instance, requires nimble throat muscles. "Singing is like a sport or anything else," he said. "You have to practice. If you don't do that, it makes it tough to use those muscles."

For his gig in Baltimore, Foreaker practiced by singing in his car, alone, getting his ear trained to the song. He also practiced what he called the "phraseology" of the song, or how certain words are pronounced in order to flow into one another. At the same time, he tried not to practice to the point where singing the song became mechanical. He said a good performance needs to be fresh, not tired and by rote. He does not believe in fiddling with the song. "Just go out there and sing the thing. Don't monkey with it too much."

He said some singers definitely do a better job than others.

"Boyz II Men sang it and they were incredible," he recalled. "And then there's some performers you can hardly sit through." As for Roseanne Barr's infamous crotch-grabbing incident some years ago, he said, "What did anyone expect? That's part of her *shtick*."

Being asked to sing the anthem at the Orioles ballpark is no small accomplishment. According to Monica Pence, communications manager for the Orioles, the team receives hundreds of applications from potential anthem singers around the world. With about eighty home games slated, only a small percentage of would-be anthem singers are chosen.

Candidates submit a resume of their singing experience and also a tape of themselves singing the anthem. Members of the Ballpark Entertainment Production staff review the applications and choose the anthem singers for the upcoming season. Preference is given to Marylanders. "We have some famous people singing, but since it is the hometown team, we try to have some local people sing it," she said.

The Orioles aren't the only baseball team to seek out local talent for singing the anthem. Every August, the Philadelphia Phillies hold public tryouts for would-be anthem singers. On the Philadelphia news one night a parade of anthem singers gave it a try. One young man in a backward baseball cap took a Frank Sinatra-meets-Harry Connick Jr. approach. It was the national anthem lounge act. One group gave the anthem a gospel sound and then a Diana Ross wannabe hit all her high notes for the camera.

In Baltimore, one of the locals the Orioles selected to sing was Tamara Walker, a Maryland native who now lives in Los Angeles. Her music has been in soundtracks for the films *Coyote Ugly* and *Angel Eyes.*

Walker sang the spring evening that I watched the Orioles—or "O's" as they're known in Baltimore—play the

New York Yankees. Summer had come early to Oriole Park at Camden Yards. The sun hovering above the rim of the stadium was unusually hot for early May. As the sun went down, the lights came on. The game ball was thrown out by Hasin Rahman, the Baltimore boxer who had come out of nowhere to win the world heavyweight title. "Ladies and gentlemen, please stand for our national anthem," the announcer said. "Gentlemen, please remove your hats."

Thousands of people bobbed to their feet. Fans who were already on their third or fourth beer lurched upright. Hats whipped off. And then Walker's lush voice launched into the national anthem.

Some of the baseball fans listened as if they took pride in the words of the song, written just a short distance away in the city's harbor. They stood ramrod straight like soldiers on review, hands over their hearts. Not everyone looked inspired. Other fans slouched with hands hanging at their sides or even jammed into their pockets. On the field below, the baseball players stood in orderly rows, caps over hearts.

Singing the national anthem is a particular challenge in Baltimore, where "O's" fans have claimed a part of the song as their very own. When the singer is in the home stretch, singing "*O say does that...*", the spectators shout out the "O" long and loud. It's great fun for the fans, even if they don't know the rest of the words, but it can be disconcerting to a singer. "We always tell people about the 'O' in case they haven't been out there before," Pence said. "It's kind of a fun, Baltimore crowd tradition."

On this particular night, Walker nailed it. A huge cheer went up as she sang the final words. By the time the last inning was played, the concrete steps would be sticky with spilled soda and beer, but for now the stadium was fresh, the night full of promise. The game wound on. In the fifth inning, Oriole Jeff Conine knocked a grand slam to center field and the O's pulled ahead, but they couldn't hold their lead. The Yankees won, 7 to 5. The highlight of the night was walking around to the seats behind home plate and watching Cal Ripken at bat in what would turn out to be his final season.

Baseball and the national anthem have always gone hand-in-hand. The Washington Post recently published a tongue-in-cheek editorial regarding the origins of baseball. Here is an excerpt.

Old-Timers Day

The search for the origins of baseball has now gone as far back as 1823, late in the second administration of James Monroe, who is not known ever to have thrown out an opening pitch. . . .

Others say there is evidence the national pastime has existed in one form or another since the 18th century – that something resembling it may have been played by the soldiers at Valley Forge. Perhaps so; it may even transpire that Gen. Washington occasionally paused as he passed through camp to suggest pitching the next batter high and inside or observe, "That catcher couldn't throw out Cornwallis's grandmother.". . .

Serious fans, just to put a marker somewhere, might argue that real baseball did not exist in American cities until the coming of "The Star-Spangled Banner," roasted peanuts and Casey Stengel.

The *Post* editorial writer might have added that the unofficial ending of the song is, "Play ball!" Back at Camden Yards, the Orioles spokesperson agreed that the national anthem held extra significance for fans, considering the battle for Baltimore took place barely two miles away. "The national anthem is a very important song and I think everyone respects that," Pence said. "This was a song that was born in Baltimore and so it has a special place here."

14

The Burning of Washington
A Maryland village becomes capital of the United States for a day

Route 97 winds through Brookeville, carrying commuters to downtown Washington. Following rush hour on a July morning, not much was stirring except a few customers at the post office on the corner. Hard to believe that this sleepy town was once capital of the United States—if only for a day.

Brookeville's call to duty came on August 26, 1814. With Washington in ashes and occupied by enemy troops, the president fled to a friend's home here to continue running the United States government.

This morning, there was nothing more threatening than a patch of poison ivy, which had taken root in a stone wall in front of the historic Brookeville Academy. Town resident Barbara Ray was busy trying to douse the poison ivy with weed killer. She had lived in the 200-year-old house across the street for a decade. "I think it's just like a family," she said of town living. "It *is* a village. We all know each other. Some people were born here."

That sense of community can be hard to find anymore, especially in the Washington suburbs. Brookeville has become popular with commuters seeking a quiet retreat from D.C., located eighteen miles south on Route 97. The former farms surrounding the town have long since sprouted mini-mansions that sell for $500,000 or more. "For a while, living here was affordable," said Ray, noting that home prices had soared in the last few years. "The village appeals to people. They think it's pretty."

The town incorporated in 1894 but has roots going back another century. At town meetings, residents discuss Brookeville's growing pains and weigh small changes carefully. Some townspeople were recently at odds over whether or not to replace uneven brick sidewalks with modern concrete walks. There was also some concern about a large plot for sale in town and what could be built there. Residents were hoping it wouldn't be more mini-mansions.

Most of the commuters passing through town have never been down its historic side streets, where huge trees provide shade from the July heat and the old, brick sidewalks are green with moss. A little further, on the edge of town, is a stately home. A brass plaque and a roadside historical marker overgrown with bittersweet vines are the only clues that this house once served as headquarters for the United States government in exile.

In 1814, Washington was barely more than a frontier town. Carved out of the swampy wilderness along the Potomac River in the late 1700s, the capital had been designed in a grand way by French architect Pierre L'Enfant. The unpaved avenues were muddy, pigs snuffled in the garbage and chickens scratched in the alleys. Intrepid congressmen walking from the White House to the Capitol often waded through brush growing in the middle reaches of Pennsylvania Avenue. Slaves were a common sight. Even though situated in weedy surroundings, the public buildings were large, marble and ornate.

The most magnificent building was the Capitol, designed by Benjamin Latrobe. Americans today would not recognize the building because it lacked the dome completed during Abraham Lincoln's presidency. The Senate and House chambers were linked by a wooden passageway. The chamber of the House of Representatives was octagonal and measured eighty-five feet by sixty feet. Massive columns upheld a wooden roof with one hundred skylights made of imported English glass.

No less impressive was the Library of Congress. The main room measured eighty-six feet by thirty-five feet with a thirty-six-foot-high ceiling. The library contained nearly 3,000 books that would all be lost in the fire. Many of the books had been printed in London, their pages filled with history and explanations of English law.

Washington had obvious symbolic value but it was not a city of strategic importance. There was a navy yard, but otherwise the city had no military base or any real commerce or industry. It was a city designed for the running of government. By comparison, nearby Baltimore was a thriving commercial center with a busy port where goods arrived from around the world.

Washington's lack of strategic value lulled the nation's leaders into a false sense of security. The common logic was that the British would not bother to attack Washington but would target Baltimore instead. Some politicians insisted on this viewpoint right up until the Redcoats were at the very gates.

L'Enfant had designed the streets with defense in mind. Diagonal avenues radiated from traffic circles like spokes in a wheel, cutting through the grid of streets. Artillery positioned in the circles could defend all approaches into the heart of the city. Despite L'Enfant's clever strategy, not so much as a single cannon was waiting for the British invaders.

The man in charge of defending Maryland was General William Winder. Overworked and overwhelmed, he was unable to organize a defense. Secretary of War John Armstrong was among those who insisted that Washington would not be attacked. President Madison deferred from making military decisions, claiming that he was no soldier. Ironically, Madison would soon become the only serving president ever to take up arms on a battlefield.

Leading the British troops were two very capable commanders, Admiral Cockburn and Sir Robert Ross. Ross, a hero of the Napoleonic Wars, was technically in command of the expedition. Cockburn, eager to take part in the invasion, insisted on coming along. Ross moved cautiously toward Washington, amazed that his troops were crossing enemy territory unmolested. Cockburn, always full of disdain for Americans, did his best to goad Ross on.

British forces came from two directions. By water, the British approached Washington on the Potomac River. They were amazed to discover that Fort Washington, guarding the approach to the city, had been abandoned. British officers later admitted that the fort would have been a major obstacle to the invasion. Unopposed, the British sailed on to Alexandria, where the city fathers surrendered.

On land, the second part of the British force marched toward Washington. The Americans were so intent on guarding Baltimore that they were caught off guard by the attack on the nation's capital. A hasty, last-minute attempt at defending the city became a case of too little, too late. Experienced fighters suggested that the Americans harry the British relentlessly, felling trees across the roads and ambushing the Redcoats at every opportunity. This strategy had worked well enough during the Revolutionary War. American leaders, determined to meet the British in a formal battle, refused to harass the invaders.

For the British, the biggest enemy was the Chesapeake Bay's notoriously steamy August weather. Soldiers collapsed in the heat and died of sunstroke. Most of the troops had been aboard ship for months and were in poor physical condition for marching down the sun-baked roads.

British troops finally encountered American militia at the village of Bladensburg outside Washington. Although the Americans outnumbered the British, once again the militia was no match for seasoned Redcoats.

President Madison had ridden out from the White House to inspire the troops. At one point before the shooting began, Madison galloped toward the bridge leading into Bladensburg, dueling pistols strapped to his waist. Alarmed, an officer ran out just in time to warn the president that the British already occupied the town. Madison quickly turned around.

The president made no attempt to lead the battle, aside from making a few suggestions to his commanders. Secretary of War Armstrong was also present, and Madison asked him if he had any advice for General Winder on the placement of troops. Armstrong had already informed Madison that the American militia would lose against British regulars. Armstrong, the author of a book on military strategy entitled, *Hints to Young Generals*, did not offer any to Winder.

General Winder set the stage for an American defeat when he went out of his way to describe lines of retreat to his officers rather than encouraging them to hold against the British. Secretary of State James Monroe muddled the situation even further when, in an effort to help General Winder, he mistakenly ordered troops to the wrong position.

The battle began before either side was ready to fight. Skirmishers opened fire, the distant pop, pop, pop of muskets carrying across the Anacostia River. Over-eager British officers led a charge directly into the American artillery, when a flanking movement would have been more effective and might have saved British lives. The sight of bayonets gleaming in the sun was too much for skittish American militia, already eager to retreat. The Americans fled so quickly that the battle would come to be nicknamed "the Bladensburg races."

Among the few Americans who did not run was Commodore Joshua Barney. Barney commanded a crew of sailors that included several free African-Americans, the sight of whom took President Madison by surprise. Upon reviewing Barney's men before the fight, the president asked the commodore, "if his negroes would not run on the approach of the British?"

"No sir," Barney replied. "They don't know how to run. They will die by their guns first."

Barney's boast to the president was true. The experienced navy gunners ravaged the oncoming Redcoats. His sailors kept loading and firing until they were cut down by British bayonets. Barney, badly wounded, told his men to leave him. Several sailors refused to do so and were captured with their commodore.

Barney and his tiny naval force had long been a crafty British adversary on Chesapeake Bay. His reputation, along with his bravery at Bladensburg, impressed the professional soldiers who captured him.

"I regret to see you in this state, Commodore," Admiral Cockburn reportedly said upon meeting Barney. The wounded commodore was immediately paroled and carried away to receive medical care.

The battle left fifty-six Redcoats dead and nearly 200 wounded; most of them fell before Commodore Barney's guns. The Americans lost about fifty dead and wounded, with 150 captured by the British in the ensuing retreat.

The British did not stay long in Bladensburg but pushed on toward the American capital. At the White House, with the president away at the battlefield, first lady Dolley Madison packed what valuables she could. She ordered the full-length portrait of George Washington cut from its frame and saved from the invaders.

Except for a few servants, the first lady was left to fend for herself. As the British approached, Mrs. Madison dashed off a letter to her sister,

> I have pressed as many Cabinet papers into trunks as to fill one carriage. Our private property must be sacrificed, as it is impossible to procure wagons for its transportation. I am determined not to go myself until I see Mr. Madison safe, so that he can accompany me, as I hear of much hostility towards him. Disaffection stalks around us. My friends and acquaintances are all gone, even Colonel C. with his hundred, who were stationed as a guard in this inclosure. French John (Dolley's faithful servant), with his usual activity and resolution, offers to spike the cannon at the gate, and lay a train of powder, which would blow up the British, should they enter the house. To the last proposition I positively object, without being able to make him understand why all advantages in war may not be taken.

The hostility toward the Madisons was real enough. Upon fleeing Washington, Mrs. Madison would be told to leave a house where she sought refuge. The angry owner blamed President Madison for putting her own husband in danger fighting the British. As night fell, Mrs. Madison was forced to find shelter elsewhere.

The Redcoats were in Washington by 8:00 PM. They found a city that was all but abandoned. A few American thieves were already busy looting the empty homes of the wealthy. Cockburn ordered his Marines to break down the doors of the United States House of Representatives. The admiral and his men then wandered around the House chamber, admiring the ornate surroundings. Cockburn plunked himself down in the speaker's chair and called out, "Shall this harbor of Yankee democracy be burned? All for it will say 'aye!'" His men gave a cheer, then began piling furniture for the bonfire. Flames soon spread through the House and Senate.

The British then moved on to the deserted president's house. The contents of the White House became spoils of war. Ross and Cockburn were amazed to find the dining room set for what was to have been the president's victory feast. The Redcoats helped themselves to the food and wine, drinking to the health of the king. Cockburn took a cushion from Dolley Madison's chair as a keepsake, crudely joking about possessing the first lady's "seat." Dinner over, they put the president's house to the torch.

Soon the White House, Capitol and Library of Congress were burning, along with other public buildings. More of the city might have been lost if a storm had not blown up that night, dousing the fires. The flames were visible from as far away as Baltimore, where the residents worried that they might be next.

The destruction continued the following day. More buildings were burned, including the War Department and offices of the Secretary of State. That afternoon, a hurricane off Chesapeake Bay struck the city with tremendous winds, rain and lightning that seemed like some awful reckoning. Gusts blew so hard that marauding Redcoats were knocked off their feet. More bad luck befell the British when a well packed with captured American gunpowder exploded, killing thirty men and wounding fourty-seven.

On Thursday night, the British moved out. General Ross was reluctant to spend another night in the burned ruins of Washington. His small force, battered by the elements, was in hostile territory. He knew that if the American militia managed to organize an attack, the Redcoats might face disaster. The British returned to their waiting ships under cover of darkness.

In Brookeville, President Madison was settling into his temporary headquarters. Madison stayed at the home of the town postmaster, Caleb Bentley. Members of his cabinet found lodging at other houses in town. The United States government had reached its most vulnerable moment, yet it somehow managed to endure and function out of the postmaster's house.

In the aftermath, some British officers reported being sickened by the wanton destruction at Washington. When news of the sack of Washington reached London there was, at first, a general celebration. A more sober reaction soon followed to the burning of the public buildings and the thousands of books at the Library of Congress.

For more than a century it was thought that no books had survived, but in 1940 a collector made an interesting gift to the library. On the first page of the book, in Cockburn's handwriting, was a notation that the lone volume had been taken by the admiral as a souvenir of the library's destruction in 1814.

Some officials in the British government declared that while capturing the American capital was commendable, putting the city to the torch had been an act better suited to barbarians. In the United States, the burning of Washington had an unintended effect. The destruction of the city galvanized Americans against the British. After August 1814, even Americans who had opposed the war were now determined to beat the British at any cost.

For now, Americans had to rebuild on the ashes of their capital city. There was some talk of giving up on this rural outpost and moving the seat of government to Philadelphia or New York, but that smacked too much of defeat. President

Madison set the example by taking up residence in the so-called "Octagon House," a few hundred yards from the ruins of the presidential mansion. He and the first lady were living there six months later when peace was declared.

Returning to the city burned by the British was heartbreaking for most residents. "I cannot tell you what I felt on re-entering it," Dolley Madison sadly recalled. "Such destruction—such confusion."

15

The Battle of Caulk's Field

*A moonlit fight brings victory to the Eastern Shore,
tragedy to the British*

Up until late summer of 1814, the British were winning the war in the Chesapeake Bay region. Blackened timbers and cracked foundation stones were all that remained of several waterfront villages and plantations. Washington was in ashes and Baltimore would soon be under attack. The Chesapeake was as firmly in British control as the king's bathtub.

The turning point for American fortunes on the Chesapeake Bay was the battle of Caulk's Field in Kent County. In one summer night, the British would lose more than a dozen men, a British peer and their firm grasp on Maryland's bay country. American militia finally stood against disciplined British troops—and won.

Caulk's Field has all the elements of a good story, including a handsome young British captain, a fateful love letter, a moonlit battlefield, and citizen-soldiers summoned from their farms and villages to fight the invaders. If the battle had been larger, someone surely would have made a movie about it by now.

Situated far off the beaten path in the least-populated county in Maryland, Caulk's Field may be one of the most unspoiled privately owned battlefields in the United States. Trees grow in the same woods that British troops used as a shortcut, walking right into an American ambush. The brick house that was there in 1814 stands watch at the edge of battlefield. Corn is still grown on the field where soldiers bled and died. The roads that Americans and British marched down that hot August night are paved now, though lightly traveled, and a single, modern house has been built within sight of the battlefield.

Can what happened here be called a battle? It certainly was just that to the 350 or so troops who fought at this place. Fifteen British seamen and marines were killed and twenty-seven men were wounded. The British commander, Captain Sir Peter Parker, a dashing aristocrat and well-loved officer who was just twenty-eight years old, was mortally wounded. The Americans had three men wounded.

When I began to research Caulk's Field, it soon became clear that there was little in the way of an official account of this small battle. Most of what was known about the fight came from local lore and a roadside historical marker that gave the wrong information. One name kept coming up whenever I started asking about Caulk's Field. Several area residents said, "You have to talk to Stan Quick."

So that's just what I did, calling him out of the blue on a Sunday afternoon. After I explained my project, he generously agreed to help me unravel the truth about Caulk's Field and the War of 1812 on Chesapeake Bay.

One thing you soon learn about Stanley Quick, Ph.D, a seventy-something retired naval architect for Westinghouse, is that he has an engineer's attention to detail. Early in his research into the particulars of the battle, he uncovered several local legends about Caulk's Field that simply were not borne out by the facts. "Just because you read it in a history book doesn't mean it's not wrong," Quick explained, sharing his low opinion of several regional books on the history of 1812 on the Chesapeake Bay and singling out one in particular that had sold rather well. "It was just full of absolute baloney."

He arranged to meet me at the battlefield on a Saturday morning in January. When the weather forecast the night before was threatening snow, I called to see if he might want to reschedule. "Let's get this done!" he said, with all the forcefulness of one of those British officers from 1812. We agreed to meet even earlier than planned so that I could beat the snowstorm on my eighty-mile round trip. Right on schedule, I arrived at the cornfield the next morning, pulling up in my tiny Saturn behind his late-model Cadillac. After a quick handshake, he did not waste time on small talk but plunged right into giving me a tour of the battlefield. The sound of distant gunfire from goose hunters in the surrounding fields created appropriate background noise.

Quick grinned, "Just like 1814."

First stop was a granite monument erected in 1902 at the edge of the battlefield. Rough stone steps led up the steep bank above the road to the monument, which marked the mass grave of at least six British sailors and marines buried on the battlefield. A four-foot-high stone wall half-circled the monument; the wall in turn was ringed by pink Rose of Sharon bushes, bare now in winter. Across the road was a well-kept farmette with a modern ranch house and a field of goats. A kennel of small dogs yapped madly at us as we climbed the steps. Otherwise, the place was deserted. An inscription was carved into the monument.

The British commanded by Sir Peter Parker Baronet and the Americans Commanded by Col. Philip Reed met in engagement on this field August 31st, 1814. The British were defeated and Sir Peter Parker killed.

Erected A.D. 1902 by Marylanders to commemorate the

Patriotism and fortitude of the victor and vanquished.

Back in July, in a season closer to the one in which the soldiers fought than this winter's day, I had visited the same spot. Then, as now, I felt uneasy thinking about the men buried here. This lonely location was custom made for hauntings. Judging by the beer bottles splashed around the monument, it was also a popular hangout for the rural party crowd.

During my summertime visit, it was impossible to see the battlefield on account of the corn, a modern hybrid that grows much taller than its nineteenth century counterpart. Now, under leaden skies and chilled by a damp wind that promised snow, Quick pointed out where the two forces were positioned on a bare field spiked with corn stubble.

What I had not seen in July were two low hills or ridges that were crucial during the battle. These ridges ran almost parallel to each other, like rolling waves, separated by a few hundred feet of corn field. Quick also showed me a wooded area that had been there in 1814. The patch of woods resembled a beach that the twin ridges in the field were rolling toward. British marines had come rushing out of these same woods in the moonlight, straight into an ambush set by the Americans.

Patiently, Quick explained how the battle came about. After raiding up and down the Chesapeake Bay in 1813, the British turned deadly serious about the war in the summer of 1814. On August 24, British troops put Washington to the torch. The White House and Capitol building went up in flames. Baltimore would be the next target.

The British invasion plan included diversionary attacks against the Eastern Shore on the opposite side of the bay. The man sent to harass the upper bay was Captain Sir Peter Parker. "They were ordered to wreak havoc," Quick explained. "They were ordered to prevent any reinforcements from crossing the bay. He was sent to be as annoying as he could."

Parker was a well-connected rising star in the Royal Navy. His wife was related to Lord Byron, the famed poet. He held the hereditary title of baronet, marking him as a member of the British ruling class.

Parker's ship, the frigate *HMS Menelaus,* was accompanied by several smaller vessels. No American ship had any hope of standing up to *Menelaus.* For Chesapeake Bay residents, the massive war ship was the nineteenth century equivalent of Darth Vader's *Death Star.* The ship was a floating fortress from which the British launched their raids. By late August, *Menelaus* was anchored off Fairlee Creek with its guns trained on a waterfront plantation owned by a family named Waller.

Fairlee Creek is a sleepy, tea-colored waterway edged with woods, fields and eighteenth century plantation homes. Parker found easy pickings among these rich plantations. British raiding parties carried off wine, ham and chickens, salted fish and smoked oysters. The raiders burned whatever they could not take with them, including storage barns and the genteel old houses.

By the time the local militia saw smoke rising on the horizon, the British raiders had already returned to their frigate. These hit-and-run tactics proved as frustrating to the militia as they were successful for the British.

Finally, on August 30, the tables turned in favor of the Kent County militia. Colonel Philip Reed was camped with half his regiment three miles inland on a field surrounded by woods. It was a typical muggy August night, when even darkness did not bring much relief from the heat and humidity.

After so much abuse at the hands of the British raiders,

Reed was probably frustrated and spoiling for a fight. He had with him 174 men of the 21st Regiment of the Maryland Militia—mostly townspeople and farmers, certainly not disciplined troops such as the British had. Since the beginning of the war, there had been several alarms about British raiders, but so far the militia had never met the enemy.

At age fifty-four, Reed was an experienced leader. He had fought in the Revolutionary War and served as a United States senator. That night he would prove he was both capable and lucky.

Aboard the *Menelaus*, Sir Peter was busy writing a prophetic note to his wife in England.

H.M.S. Menelaus
August 30th 1814
My Darling Marianne:
I am just going on desperate service and entirely depend upon valor and example for its successful issue. If anything befalls me I have made a sort of will. My country will be good to you and our adored children. God Almighty bless and protect you all. Adieu, most beloved Marianne, adieu!
Peter Parker
P.S. I am in high health and spirits

According to Quick, Sir Peter knew what he was getting into. He had heard about the militia camp and intended to fight and capture as many of the Americans as he could. "Parker made up his mind he was going to catch what he believed was an entire regiment," Quick said.

Parker reportedly said he was anticipating "a frolic with the Yankees." That's not as light-hearted as it sounds. Quick pointed out that the word "frolic" had a different meaning in 1814 from the word today. It meant a brutal fight, which was just what Parker got.

From the *Menelaus*, boats launched in the moonlight and carried as many as 170 British troops ashore. It was supposed to be a surprise attack, but the raiders soon stumbled across American pickets, who fired on the British. "Everybody heard those shots," Quick said. "The game was up."

The American militia rushed to meet the raiders. Both sides stumbled toward each other across the dark woods and fields. The British were guided by a slave they had liberated from a local plantation. The slave led them toward the American camp, which was five miles from the landing site. Meanwhile, the Americans were heading for the area where they had heard the pickets' shots.

The Americans would have been cut off from their camp and artillery by the British force if it had not been for two visiting militia members who went scouting on their own and found the raiders on a back road. The scouts hurried to alert their comrades and the Americans returned just in time to take up positions in the corn field near their camp.

In setting the stage for the battle, Reed made several smart moves. First, he felled trees across a narrow road or "cut" through the woods to slow down the British troops. Next, where the road came out of the woods and crossed the field on Caulk's farm, he hid about twenty riflemen in the corn. Reed had the rest of his men form a line on the first ridge in the field, where his artillery was also placed.

"Peter Parker, being very arrogant, and brave, went through the cut," Quick said. As the first group of British marines finished climbing over the felled trees, they were ambushed by the Americans. Most of the British who died in the battle fell at that spot.

Reed immediately returned to the first ridge as the British formed a line and charged up the hill toward the militia's cannons. "When they got close enough, Reed opened up with his guns," Quick said.

American muskets and artillery cut the British to pieces, killing and wounding several men, included a midshipman killed at the forefront of the attack. Musket fire continued as both sides tried to gain the upper hand. Lead balls whipped and snicked through the corn stalks. Smoke hung thick and hazy. The British each carried about forty rounds of ammunition while the Americans had only about half that amount. Alarmed that his men were running low on ammunition, Reed ordered the militia to fall back to the second ridge, where they formed again. His plan was to fight a rearguard action with some of his troops, while the rest of the militia fled. He told the men who had ammunition to give it to those staying behind to fight.

The second British attack never came. "Peter Parker was killed right where we're standing," Quick said. The first flakes of snow from the coming storm were falling, adding a chill to Quick's words. He pointed toward the woods. "They took his body down to that side of the field and they laboriously carried Peter Parker back over the tree trunks."

Suffering thirty percent casualties, their gallant young captain dead, and in peril at any moment of being ambushed again by American militia, the British made their way back to *Menelaus*. They carried Parker on their shoulders, stopping on occasion so a new detail of men could take on the weight. In this way they crossed five miles of unfamiliar territory at night in the sweltering heat. At one point, they were attacked by American militia cavalry. Fortunately for the British, the militia ran off as the Redcoats returned fire with the last of their ammunition. Upon reaching the waterfront, the British had trouble finding the landing boats they had hidden there. They finally returned to *Menelaus* around 4:00 AM, battered and exhausted.

In his official report of the battle, Colonel Reed wrote,

You will be surprised, Sir, when I inform you that in an engagement of so long continuance, in an open field, when the moon shone brilliantly on the rising ground occupied by our troops, while the shade of the neighboring woods under the protection of which the enemy fought gave us but an indistinct view of anything but the flash of his guns, that under the disparity of numbers against us, and the advantage of regular discipline on the side of the enemy we had not one man killed, and only one sergeant, one corporal and one private wounded, and those slightly.

Roots run deep in Kent County, a place where nobody qualifies as a "local" unless his parents and grandparents were born there too. Many longtime residents are descended from 1812 veterans. One family even has Colonel Reed's sword all these years later.

In a strip of greenery along High Street in Chestertown, the county seat, there is a series of monuments to local soldiers, beginning with the Revolutionary War, then 1812, right on up to the Persian Gulf War. The monument honoring Civil War veterans has one side with the list of those who fought for the Union, while the other side names those who fought for the Confederacy. A monument added many years later honors African-American Civil War soldiers from Kent County.

"It is the only time the Maryland militia stood and fought," said Stewart Barroll, a Chestertown attorney whose ancestor fought with the American militia at Caulk's Field. Barroll has a real love for local history and is an active Civil War re-enactor. "The *Menelaus* was participating in hit and run vandalism," he explained. "What Peter Parker was doing was trying to play with the militia. He was looking for a fight. He was just trying to have a little fun. But number one, they were ready for him, and number two, they fought.

"There was a trail through the woods and the British came out right on the field under the full moon," he said. "They were actually able to see the Americans lined up in the moonlight."

The Barroll family's roots go all the way back to the Rev. William Barroll, who arrived from England in 1760. The War of 1812 veteran in the family was Barroll's great-great-great grandfather James Edmondson Barroll, who attended both Washington College in Chestertown and Yale University. He served as the secretary and adjutant of the Troop of Horse of the Kent County Militia.

The descendants of other 1812 veterans are common enough today. "It's literally like looking in the Kent County phone directory," Barroll said, noting that only a handful of area residents are interested in the history of the battle. Later, during the Civil War, families that had once fought together became enemies. Barroll related to me the tragic story of his great-great grandfather, who, despite his family's patriotic heritage, became a victim of oppression during the Civil War when he spoke up for state's rights. Barroll's ancestor was the state's attorney for Kent County and also editor of the weekly *Kent Conservator* newspaper, which took a pro-Southern viewpoint.

When the *Conservator* reprinted an editorial from another newspaper in April 1863 which criticized the suspension of *habeas corpus*, there was trouble. Union soldiers steamed up the Chester River, marched to the newspaper office, and gave the editor one hour to settle his affairs. He was then escorted to the waterfront, put aboard the ship, and taken to Fort McHenry in Baltimore, where he was locked in a cell beside the sallyport. Visitors today can see these damp, cramped cells with the barred doors. After being imprisoned there for three nights, he was put on a Baltimore & Ohio Railroad train that took him the length of Maryland to Confederate territory.

"Basically, he was shipped off and told never to return," Barroll said. He added that the rival newspaper in Chestertown was thrilled. "The *Kent County News* was just cackling."

There was nothing funny about it for Barroll's great-great grandfather, especially when news came that his little girl had died at Christmastime in 1864 while he was banished. "He was terribly bitter toward the Union Army authorities," Barroll said.

The exiled Barroll was able to return after the war, having paid a heavy price for practicing his right to free speech. It was another ugly incident during a dark time in an area where loyalties were divided.

According to H. Hurtt Derringer, long-time editor of the *Kent County News,* the same newspaper that had a laugh over the fate of a rival editor in 1863, interest in what happened at Caulk's Field has ebbed and flowed over the years like the Eastern Shore's tidal rivers.

"I'd say there's not as much interest in the last decade or so," said Derringer, now retired, who can give a good recounting of the battle. "Peter Parker supposedly said he would eat his breakfast in Chestertown or hell . . . the militia were in the moonlight, just waiting for them."

Over the years, Caulk's Field has received little mention. The *Baltimore Sun* did report on the rededication of the battlefield monument in its September 13, 1967 edition. Money for fixing up the monument, a sum of sixty dollars, had been raised by members of the Caulk's Field 4-H Chapter.

Sun reporter Earl Arnett waxed eloquent on the subject.

Last Saturday Kent Countians again lined up in front of

the marker in a dedication ceremony for the refurbished memorial. Automobiles, instead of the carriages of the 1902 ceremony, lined the country road just off Route 21. Soldiers in starched khakis, a detail from the Tolchester Nike missile base, stood by in silent poses of dutiful attention. Boy Scouts from Chestertown were there, and representatives from the segregated American Legion posts from Chestertown. . . . The scene was vintage American and seemed to have an elusive significance beyond the fact of a few people gathered in front of an isolated monument on a country road.

Even today, this emptiness is what makes Kent County such a beautiful and relatively undiscovered place. The genteel old farmhouses and rich colonial history give the area an oddly English feel. You halfway expect people to have a British accent, but they sound pretty much like everyone else except for the occasional old-timer who speaks the local dialect known as "Delmarvese."

One place I sought out that definitely feels Old World is St. Paul's Episcopal Church, established in 1692. Local legend says that War of 1812 militia once spent the night inside the church because of the threat of thunderstorms. All the doors were open to lessen the August heat, and a flock of sheep wandered into the church as the men slept. The sheep supposedly woke the men, causing some excitement when the sleepy soldiers mistook the sheep for British invaders. I always thought it was a good anecdote, and it may even be true.

With help from my wife and children, I explored the church and grounds one summer afternoon. Located just a short march from Caulk's Field, the brick church was built in 1713 and is surrounded by several ancient trees, including a gigantic southern magnolia. This is the upper northern range for this species, so perhaps the nearby bay tempers the winters. Several large spruces also ring the church yard. Two trees that were certainly there in 1812—at least they must have been tall enough to escape that hungry flock of foraging sheep—were a massive European or common linden tree, identified with help from my wife the horticulturist, and a truly aged swamp chestnut oak. A brass plaque from 1976 at the base of the oak identified it as an official Bicentennial Tree. I took a snapshot of our children at the base of the tree and they looked tiny as twin squirrels beside the enormous, gnarled trunk.

Even older than the trees were some of the headstones. We came across a weathered lump of rock identified by a more modern stone as belonging to Michael Miller 1624-1699, "Donor of this churchyard." Some of the other older stones that could be read marked the graves of Thomas Wickers 1783-1863, James Lamb 1818-1880 and a Sarah Richard, who died at "61 yrs of age" in 1812.

There was one more old headstone—more like a tablet—with an epitaph that gives visitors something to reflect upon. The long-ago words also put local history in perspective. The stone was so old that the letter "s" was carved in an "f" shape in colonial fashion.

Here lyes ye boddy
of Danniel Coley.
He departed this life
October ye 20. 1729
Cut by John Godffrey

Behold and see nowhere I Lye
As you are now so once was I
As I am now so must you be
Therefore prepare to follow me

Snow began to whiten the blacktop as Stan Quick and I left the battlefield. We stopped to gas up at a lonely roadside establishment called the Caulk's Field One Stop. Signs out front advertised, "Gas • Diesel • Kero • Fresh Coffee" —but no battlefield souvenirs.

Driving on, Quick was generous enough to show me his beautiful home on Fairlee Creek. As we arrived, he gave the stately brick house a perfunctory wave. "Welcome to Carvill Hall," he said.

Built in 1695 as the home of the Lord High Sheriff, it is the oldest house in Kent County and also the birthplace of 1812 veteran Major Thomas Carvill. Quick and his wife bought the house in 1985 and have done extensive work since then. We went inside, knocking the fresh snow from our boots. Superlatives fall short in describing this house. Antiques, ship models in glass cases and old oil paintings fill the rooms. There was a painting of a British earl in the dining room.

"People always think it's one of my ancestors," Quick joked. In an upstairs hallway in front of the stairs leading to the third floor was another portrait, a copy of an original oil painting of the youthful Peter Parker. "He was quite a young man," Quick said. "This was painted about three years before he was killed."

Perhaps the *piece de resistance* of Quick's art collection was a large oil painting he commissioned a British artist to paint depicting *HMS Menelaus* in the Chesapeake Bay off Fairlee Creek. The wonderfully detailed painting will eventually be used for the cover art of the book Quick is writing about the history of the War of 1812 on Chesapeake Bay. Much of the manuscript is complete, but Quick speculated that he has a few years of work left. He has spent countless hours on the project, writing either with papers spread out on a large table in a sunroom overlooking Fairlee

Creek or in an office at one end of the house.

His fascination with 1812 began in the 1980s, when he was having renovation work done to his home. Records showed there also had been extensive work done about 1818. "It occurred to me that they likely did renovations because, like us, they had to."

Quick speculated that damage done during the British raids might have prompted the repair work. Although he can't prove it, his guess is that the house might even have been hit by an errant Congreve rocket during an attack on a neighboring home. "I never did learn much about what happened to the house," he said. But he did begin to piece together a history of 1812, starting with Caulk's Field, then moving on to documenting the whole Chesapeake Bay campaign.

Quick's work is the result of meticulous research. When I called to set up our meeting, he had been excited after making a discovery while reading the account of a British marine who had fought at Caulk's Field. It described the "cut" through the woods, something which had puzzled Quick because it was referred to in an account of the battle written years later as a defile, or a sunken road. There was no such road there. The marine had phrased it in simple terms and his memory was fresh: they had passed through a "cut" through the woods. For historians, small discoveries like this are priceless.

"It's virtually a labor of love to translate what is written because the handwriting is so tough," Quick said. "It is so tedious to get the materials and transcribe them."

"Ground Zero" for him has been the logs of more than fifty ships from the upper bay in the 1812 era. "I'm sitting here looking at four volumes of ship's logs right now," he said.

Besides deciphering the old-fashioned handwriting, he noted another roadblock to modern historians is that the meanings of words have changed since the early nineteenth century—such as that word "frolic" that Parker used in anticipating his fight with the Yankees. "Annoy" is another word that pops up in British orders. Today a fly in your bedroom might annoy you, but in 1812 annoy had a harsher meaning: to harass or attack and *do damage.* To help his readers, Quick has compiled a 250-term glossary to go with the book.

The Kent County newspapers of that era were lost in a fire, so he had turned to newspapers such as the *Niles Weekly Register* and *National Intelligencer* for contemporary accounts. Another bit of light reading had been Henry Adams' nine-volume history of the United States, which includes three volumes just on the administration of President James Madison.

He also had spent time researching and disproving some of the anecdotes that have come down through the years about Caulk's Field. For example, there was a legend that Sir Peter Parker's body was pickled in a barrel of rum and shipped back to England for burial. Quick said it simply wasn't true. A similar legend has the body of Sir Robert Ross, killed at the battle of North Poin, being pickled in a cask of Madeira. It is likely these stories gathered steam in local lore because it's such an ignominious ending for the evil British invader after being shot down by the American militia.

According to Quick, Parker was put in a lead coffin and buried temporarily in Bermuda before being exhumed for reburial in England. Similarly, the young English midshipman cut down by American grapeshot at Caulk's Field and buried there was dug up by family members and reburied in England.

Quick also does not put much stock at all in the legendary claim by Sir Peter: "I'll eat breakfast in Chestertown or hell!"

"Some general is always supposedly saying 'I'll eat breakfast in so-and-so or hell,'" Quick said. "I'm sure someone did in fact make that claim, but not everyone could have said it."

For Quick, history is clearly serious business. In his manuscript, he said he strove for primary sources with each paragraph, or, if using secondary sources, he tried to verify the information. What couldn't be verified, he left out. To him, it was a simple process but very time consuming. He noted that other authors had cranked out several alleged "history books" while he was working on this one.

"I gave a talk about my book, and I told people it was easy to write one. Just give yourself fifteen years and $50,000," he said. He does manage to keep a sense of humor about how many people will actually be interested in reading the book or in learning more about 1812. "There's a certain level of interest, but not much." He has given talks where as many as one hundred people came. "It probably totals ten people in Kent County who have a real interest. I figure if I mention all the towns along the bay, about ten people in each town will buy a book," he speculated, tongue in cheek. "Before long I'll have sold a thousand copies!"

16

By Dawn's Early Light
Fort McHenry and the Battle of Baltimore

Deep inside the walls of Fort McHenry, it was as damp and cool as the salt-washed breeze off Baltimore harbor. Water dripped from between cracks in the mortar of the arched brick ceiling, spattering visitors filing through the dark doorway. This room had served many purposes over the years, from powder magazine to prison.

This was a place for conjuring history—and defiant spirits.

"We call it America's forgotten war," said Fort McHenry National Park Ranger Vincent Vaise. "Most Americans really don't know much about the war or what happened here at the fort."

The battle for Baltimore fought at Fort McHenry was America's great moment in the Chesapeake Bay campaign during the War of 1812. The victory over the British invaders gave the United States new hope, a national anthem, and a flag known as the Star-Spangled Banner.

In our post 9-11 world, it does not take much imagination to realize how nervous the residents of Baltimore must have felt in 1814, when British forces intent on burning the city prepared to attack. One of my visits to Fort McHenry took place just five days after the September 11, 2001 terrorist attack. Every overpass on I-95 had a flag flying from it. Hand-made banners proclaimed *God bless America* or even *Honk 4*

USA. In every public place the air was tangy with patriotism—and fear over what might happen next.

Back in September 1814, there must have been a similar mixture of patriotic feeling and anxiety as citizens rushed to defend their homes. City residents tried to sift the news from the rumors spreading in the streets in those days before CNN brought live television coverage into every living room. The full might of the British military was about to be unleashed on soldiers who, until a few days earlier, had been farmers, storekeepers and schoolboys.

Nearly two centuries later, the spacious grounds overlooking the entrance to Baltimore harbor are usually dotted with people flying kites and lovers lounging on blankets. Older couples bring lawn chairs to sit in the shade and chat as they watch passing boats.

"People go to places like Yellowstone and they are expecting something, maybe solitude, but there are too many people, or they go to Gettysburg and there are too many monuments and they can't see the battlefield and they are disappointed," Vaise said. "When visitors come here they really don't know what to expect and they are pleasantly surprised. It's a national treasure."

At first, the fort looks too small to have generated such a big legend. Inside the five-sided, star-shaped fortress, a series of exhibits in the old troop barracks give an overview of life at the fort through the years well beyond 1812. The whole tour can easily be done in less than an hour if you don't pause too long in any one particular spot.

According to Vaise, the fort's visitors generally fall into two categories. "One group knows there was a War of 1812 and not much beyond that," he said. "The other group doesn't even know there was a War of 1812."

Vaise said visitors often have their wars and their history mixed up. Some visitors think the War of 1812 came about because England wanted its former colonies back. Another misconception is that Betsy Ross sewed the Star-Spangled Banner and that it flew over Fort Sumter when the first shots of the Civil War were fired.

When asked why there is so much confusion about the War of 1812, he said, "The causes of the war were so much more complicated. At least with the Civil War, the causes seemed more apparent. The Revolutionary War, I think, is ingrained in the American psyche, but the War of 1812 doesn't really have that."

Vaise said that visitors who come from far away are generally more aware of the fort's history and have made it a destination. Marylanders, on the other hand, often take the fort for granted. "There are people who have lived their whole lives on Fort Avenue right down the street who have never been here," he said.

Another park ranger working to educate visitors about the fort and its role in 1812 is Scott Sheads, who leads the popular "flag talk" program. Tall, lean and bearded, Sheads is part historian, part showman as he introduces people to the story of Fort McHenry. During my visit, Sheads quickly gathered visitors on the parade green for some hands-on history. He produced a full-size nylon replica of the original Star-Spangled Banner and invited everyone to grab an edge and begin unrolling it. Touching the flag gives a better sense of its enormity. No wonder it was visible from several miles away on Chesapeake Bay. While visitors get a feel for the flag, Sheads delivers a talk that mixes history with humor, sharing the story of the fort and its famous banner.

When Sheads finished, a group of perfect strangers struggled to get the flag back into its storage bag. Taming 1,260 square feet of billowing red, white and blue fabric was no easy task. Under Sheads' direction, the participants approached the job with a surprising degree of seriousness.

This is *the flag*, they seemed to be thinking. Beside me, a man hurried to answer his cell phone as he took part in the flag-rolling operation. "I'm busy right now," he said curtly to the caller, then hung up and jammed the phone into his pocket to free up both hands for the flag.

"Make sure you've got your wedding ring on," Sheads warned. "You wouldn't believe the things—well, I could tell some stories. Last week, I heard a commotion while we were doing this and thought it was just some people being particular. Well, there was a British gent, and his tie was caught."

When the British attacked Baltimore, they had their eyes on a great prize. Baltimore was the third largest city in the United States at the time. Not only was it a commercial center in 1814, but Baltimore was the home port for a fleet of privateer vessels that harassed British shipping.

Historians Joseph A. Whitehorne and Harry L. Coles both point out in their respective books about the War of 1812 that the British never saw Baltimore as having great strategic value. By 1814, British military planners were looking toward New Orleans. That city was the key to controlling the Mississippi River and the southern states. The Chesapeake was already under British control, although the fact remained that Baltimore was the last American stronghold on the bay. Rear Admiral Sir George Cockburn fumed that Baltimore was a "nest of pirates."

The British did not expect much resistance at Baltimore. What Admiral Cockburn had seen so far of the American military had hardly struck fear in his heart. His ships traveled the Chesapeake Bay and raided waterfront towns at will. Washington had gone up in flames. Baltimore would simply be another feather in Cockburn's cap and the captured goods in the harbor would make him even richer.

After the fall of the United States capital in August, preparations for the defense of the city reached a furious pace in Baltimore. Baltimoreans were determined not to let the British sack their city.

Working in the city's favor was the fact that the local militia did not suffer from the same lack of leadership that had doomed many other American operations. One of Baltimore's leading businessmen, Militia General Samuel Smith, a Revolutionary War veteran and United States senator, put himself in charge of the city's defense. Smith was a bitter political enemy of President Madison because he believed the president was doing a poor job of running the war.

The sixty-two-year-old Smith organized the defenders with energy and savvy, cobbling together a military force and overcoming bureaucratic opposition with an iron will. He employed a silver tongue or savage threats depending on the circumstances. Smith's name and amazing leadership are mostly forgotten today in Baltimore, where Francis Scott Key is more closely associated with the battle. Without Sam Smith, however, the city probably would have fallen to the British.

The Americans lacked uniforms or even proper weapons. Many of the fort's defenders were not trained soldiers but came from the surrounding community. A wartime notice calling for recruits has been reproduced at the fort.

To reputable young men will be given a bounty of $124, and One Hundred and Sixty Acres of Land, for enlisting in the U.S. Corp of Artillery, by applying to
George Armistead
Major, Corps Artillery
Fort McHenry
Aug. 21, 1814

According to Park Ranger Vaise, soldiers who fought were given as much as 320 acres in what was then the northwestern frontier—Illinois, Indiana, Michigan and Ohio Territory. The federal government was trying to encourage the settlement of these empty territories. Vaise has visited some of these old settlements to research War of 1812 veterans from Baltimore. He found several veterans of the battle of Baltimore buried in a cemetery in Illinois.

The recruits did not get land in Maryland. "It was too valuable," Vaise said. "They didn't give it away to soldiers."

The military forces were unevenly matched, but several factors favored the Marylanders. They had General Smith. They had excellent defenses at Fort McHenry and the earthworks that Smith had ordered to be built around the city. Besides Smith, the Marylanders had other outstanding commanders: John Stricker, Oliver Hazard Perry, Fort McHenry commandant Major George Armistead and Joshua Barney, back in action after being wounded at Bladensburg. Unlike the tired American commanders early in the war, these seasoned fighters managed to combine experience and energy.

Although they were confident of victory, the British made a careful plan of attack against the city. The odds certainly favored the British. Nothing that sailed the bay could even begin to oppose the Royal Navy. Several thousand highly trained soldiers and marines, all veterans of the fight against Napoleon in Europe, were ready to face the local militia.

The attack was a combined land and sea operation of the sort that the British had become very adept at carrying out in the bay region. The plan was for a land force led by General Ross to overrun the American defenses and occupy Baltimore while the British fleet supported the land attack and made rubble out of Fort McHenry, thus opening the way for the fleet to sail into the city's harbor. The city would then be at the mercy of the British guns.

Ross went ashore with 4,000 troops on September 12, beginning what would become known as the battle of North Point. The 11,000 American troops were commanded by General Stricker, the fifty-five-year-old Revolutionary War veteran from Frederick. The Americans fell back before a series of British advances in a tactical withdrawal rather than the kind of disorganized retreat that had taken place at Bladensburg the month before. The formidable defenses built at General Smith's orders gave the militia courage.

At about 9:00 AM, when the British advance resumed, Ross rode forward to lead his troops as they once again encountered the Marylanders. It was a fateful decision. Two eighteen-year-old Baltimoreans, Daniel Wells and Harry McComas, got close enough to shoot the British officer on his white horse. Hit with buckshot and ball in the arm and chest, Ross died not far from where he fell. Vengeful British soldiers quickly turned their muskets on the two youths and killed them.

Many historians claim that the death of Ross stole the heart—and the leadership—from the British land assault. Without Ross, the British attempt to flank Fort McHenry faltered and the Redcoats bogged down. Wet weather further demoralized the British. The rain showers that had fallen all day became a heavy downpour that night. Imagine being a British soldier, your wool uniform sopping wet in Maryland's steamy late summer, fighting through soaked brush, much of your powder damp and useless, and your beloved commander dead. The Americans faced the same weather, but they were fighting for their homes and families on their own turf.

Once darkness fell, the British camped on the battlefield and licked their wounds. British losses at the battle of North Point were 38 killed, 251 wounded and 50 missing. American militia lost twenty-four killed, 139 wounded and 50 captured.

Just before dawn, as rain continued to fall, the British bombardment of Fort McHenry began. The British fleet was anchored at least two and a half miles away, out of the range of Fort McHenry's guns. The fort's garrison could only duck their heads as shells and rockets rained down.

The British attempted a sneak attack around 1:00 AM on September 14, sending boats loaded with 1,200 men ashore. When the Americans spotted the attackers' boats, batteries all along the waterfront opened fire. The element of surprise was lost and the British retreated. Out on the water, the fleet continued the bombardment.

As he watched the bombs fall, Major Armistead kept a worried eye on the fort's powder magazine, which was not bombproof and had only a shingle roof. One lucky hit would blow it up, along with most of the fort. At one point, a shell did land among the barrels of powder but by some miracle it did not explode. Having tempted fate, Armstrong ordered the barrels of powder spread throughout the fort.

Another unexploded bomb described as being "big as a flour barrel" was found to have the message *a present from the King of England* scrawled on it. The British sailors had a dark sense of humor.

During the bombardment, an estimated forty defenders were killed or wounded. One of them was a woman carrying water to thirsty artillerymen. She was disintegrated by a direct hit. Also among the dead were Lieutenant Levi Clagett and Sergeant John Clemm. Both were prosperous flour merchants. Clagett was also part owner in a Baltimore privateer. These citizen-soldiers belonged to a militia unit known as the Baltimore Fencibles. Clagett died when a British mortar shell struck his gun position. Moments later, Clemm was killed at the same spot. A chunk of shrapnel as big as a deck of cards caught him in the belly and went clear through, drilling two feet into the ground. His astonished friends later dug up the fragment.

Days after the battle, an obituary in the *Baltimore Patriot* newspaper praised the two as

> . . . men of the most amiable manners, honorable principles, and respectable standing in society. In the hour of danger they evinced ardent and collected courage.

Another defender, Lieutenant Jacob Crumbaker of the 16th Maryland Infantry, gave a lively account of the attack in a letter that is part of the park collection at Fort McHenry.

> The roaring of Cannon and the Bursting of Bombs was like one continual peal of thunder in the night. Three of their vessels Run up on the Patapsico side of the fort without being heard & when they got above the fort they gave three Cheers thinking they would throw their Bombs in Baltimore not knowing their was a little Battery above the fort but when they came even with them they let loose our Bull Dogs on their Ships and soon made them Cry for mercy and in a little time 2 of their Ship were Cut to pieces and the third made a narrow escape . . .

After nearly twenty-four hours, around seven o'clock in the morning, the tremendous bombardment ended. More than 1,800 British shells and rockets had fallen on the fort. The Star-Spangled Banner waved above the smoke and morning mist as the British fleet sailed away. On the verge of collapse from exhaustion and stress, Major Armistead turned over command of the fort to Joshua Barney and got some much-needed sleep.

Issac Munroe, an editor of the *Baltimore Patriot*

newspaper and veteran of the battle as a member of the
Baltimore Fencibles, described the moment in a September
17, 1814, letter to a friend in Boston.

> At this time our morning gun was fired, the flag hoisted,
> Yankee Doodle played, and we all appeared in full view
> of a formidable and mortified enemy, who calculated
> upon our surrender in 20 minutes after the
> commencement of the action.

Later, President Madison would issue a congratulatory
address to Baltimore, saying,

> In the varied scenes which have put to the test the
> constancy of the nation, Baltimore ranks among the
> portion most distinguished for devotion to the public
> cause that it found in the courage of its citizens a
> rampart against the assaults of an enterprising enemy . . .

The battle of Baltimore was the first and last time the fort
saw action, although for more than one hundred years it
remained a manned military post. The fort would again play
an important role in another war, this time as a prison. By
1861, a nation that had been united by a common enemy in
1812 had turned on itself and was fighting a tragic civil war in
which more than 600,000 Americans would lose their lives.

Baltimore and most of Maryland was strongly sympathetic
to the Southern cause. To prevent the state from leaving the
Union, President Abraham Lincoln and General Winfield
Scott—an aged hero of the War of 1812—acted swiftly to
occupy Maryland with Federal troops. Fort McHenry became
the prison for any city or state leaders who supported the
Confederacy. Political prisoners and Confederate soldiers
were imprisoned at a place that had once been a symbol of

freedom.

Most rank-and-file prisoners were contained in a prison camp outside the fort's walls. More important prisoners were locked within the fort. On either side of the sallyport—the fort entrance—you can visit the damp cells in which the Union's most prominent enemies were detained. These cells held Baltimore's mayor and police chief, as well as the mayor of Washington. One cell also held the grandson of Francis Scott Key.

I went into one of these prison pens, swinging open the heavy iron bars and stooping to get through the low doorway. Inside, the cell was dark and claustrophobic, with the only light coming through tiny windows set high up in the wall. The air was damp and thick.

Confederate prisoner Henry Brogden described the condition of his cell in 1863.

There was no bedstead or chair, there being no room for such luxuries. I was allowed a mattress, which I placed on the damp floor at night, and stood up on one end against the wall in the day. I was not allowed bed linen. At no time were the walls of my cell (dry), the rear wall particularly. Moisture traveled down it the whole time, and I could fill my hand with a green slime, simply by passing it up the face of the wall.

Another Confederate prisoner, captured at Gettysburg, was T.D. Witherspoon, chaplain of the 42nd Mississippi regiment. He wrote of his imprisonment at Fort McHenry,

The rancid meat and musted bread . . . were utterly destructive of health, and had we not been provided with better food through the generosity of friends in Baltimore few of us would have survived.

Another irony of Fort McHenry during the 1860s was that its commander during the War of 1812, the capable Major Armistead, had a nephew who became a Confederate general. General Lew Armistead is best known for being a leader of Pickett's Charge at Gettysburg. Paintings and illustrations portray him leading the troops with his black hat perched atop his upraised sword. Armistead and a few of his men actually made it across the killing field to reach the Union lines, an achievement that would become known as "the high water mark of the Confederacy." He was mortally wounded moments later and lies buried in the same Baltimore cemetery as his 1812 ancestor.

After the Civil War, Fort McHenry entered a slow slide into abandonment and decay. In 1905, local citizens began the effort to restore the fort, but it wasn't until 1925 that Fort McHenry became a national park.

The fort welcomes about 630,000 visitors every year. By comparison, more than 1.8 million people visit the Civil War battlefield at Gettysburg annually. In many ways, Gettysburg is the most symbolic battle of the Civil War, while Fort McHenry is likely the most symbolic battle of the War of 1812. Though located in the heart of a metropolitan area and just off Interstate 95, Fort McHenry draws far fewer visitors than its Civil War counterpart in the Pennsylvania countryside. Fort McHenry and the battle of Baltimore can not begin to compare to the human loss and horror of Gettysburg. Casualties at Baltimore totaled less than 1,000 on both sides combined. At Gettysburg, more than 50,000 Americans were killed or wounded in about the same amount of time.

Today, the harbor that the British hoped to capture has become a hub for tourism. Baltimore now ranks as the seventeenth largest city in the United States. Like any urban area, Baltimore struggles against drugs, crime and shrinking budgets. Yet Fort McHenry stands as a reminder of how citizens came together in 1814 to defend their city. Mayor Martin O'Malley often mentions Fort McHenry in speeches and recently decreed that all city government buildings would fly the fifteen-star, fifteen-stripe flag that flew above the fort during the British attack.

Speaking at the 2004 Democratic National Convention, O'Malley invoked Fort McHenry on national television. "On September 11, 1814, as Washington burned to our south during the War of 1812, the people of Baltimore—sixty percent of us immigrants, one out of five of us free black citizens of a still as yet very imperfect country—successfully defended the United States of America on our own."

Indeed, park officials noted there has been a significant increase in the number of visitors since September 11, 2001. Interest in what happened at Fort McHenry is slowly being rekindled.

Vaise, the park ranger, had a theory as to why most Americans knew so little about the fight for liberty that took place here during the War of 1812. "It shows how much we take for granted," he said. "We forget that freedom has always come with a heavy price."

17

Beginning to Forget, Beginning to Remember
James Madison's dying words and America's new destiny

News that the war was over brought the expected celebrations. In Washington, where the blackened timbers of the city poked through late winter snow, the peace treaty was especially welcome.

According to Paul Jennings,

> When the news of peace arrived, we were crazy with joy. Miss Sally Coles, a cousin of Mrs. Madison . . . came to the head of the stairs, crying out, 'Peace! Peace!' and told John Freeman (the butler) to serve out wine liberally to the servants and others. I played the President's March on the violin, John Suse' and some others were drunk for two days, and such another joyful time was never seen in Washington. Mr. Madison and all his Cabinet were as pleased as any, but did not show their joy in this manner.

At some point, President Madison must have spent some time in sober reflection. Madison had managed to stay the course and hold the nation together. Even by 1814 the young United States was a nation bursting at the seams, readying itself to spread across the vast continent to the west and rushing into the void left by old colonial powers in Louisiana and Florida.

If the War of 1812 proved anything, it was that Americans were united by common beliefs regardless of the differences in their backgrounds or geography. The United States was more than a concept in a document, it was an ideal that people believed in and lived. Nowhere else on earth could so many people have so much freedom. Unfortunately, slavery remained a stain on that ideal of freedom. The issue of slavery would go unresolved for decades.

As it passed out of living memory, the war became overshadowed by the Civil War and twentieth century wars. The fact that the War of 1812 took place when the United States was just leaving the colonial era of powdered wigs and buckled shoes makes it hard for modern Americans to relate to the events and people of the early 1800s. There were no photographs to capture images of 1812 soldiers or to document the reality of the battlefields as Matthew Brady would do during the Civil War. The War of 1812 occurred in an era portrayed in paintings and sketches; what we see has been filtered through the eyes of the artist rather than the lens of a camera. Only the rich could afford to have their portraits painted; no one recorded the faces of the everyday soldiers who shouldered a musket.

Curiously, the funeral of the last War of 1812 veteran was preserved in one of the earliest motion pictures made. Born in 1800, Hiram Cronk served in the war as a boy and died in 1905—ninety years after the war. An article in the April 26, 1903, edition of the *Sunday Utica Journal* noted that "tobacco, wine and milk are the old gentleman's steady diet . . . a gallon of wine lasts him about two weeks" and the twenty-five dollar monthly veteran's pension he received helped purchase these staples. He also had the habit of sleeping all day and pacing the floor all night. All that nicotine, alcohol and insomnia evidently helped sustain the old man to the ripe old age of

105.

His funeral was an occasion, with veterans of the Civil War taking part. As the procession passed through Brooklyn, New York, a movie camera recorded it on film, which is now available through the Library of Congress archive.

The last widow of an 1812 veteran died in 1936.

All these years later in the Chesapeake Bay region, the War of 1812 is slowly being remembered again in an official way. In June 1999, Maryland Congressman Wayne T. Gilchrest introduced legislation to begin the process of establishing a National Historic Trail to commemorate the writing of the national anthem. Called "The Star-Spangled Banner Trail," it would be one of nine national historic trails. As envisioned by Gilchrest, a Republican and decorated Vietnam War veteran who lives not far from Caulk's Field and other 1812 sites, the trail would wind through eight Maryland counties as well as Washington, D.C., and Baltimore. The trail would retrace the route of British forces in the summer of 1814, including the invasions in the Upper Chesapeake Bay in Cecil County and the battle of Caulk's Field in Kent County. The trail will include the burning of the U.S. Capitol and the White House, along with Fort McHenry and the battle of Baltimore.

"The bill offers a unique opportunity to teach each generation about the incredible events during the War of 1812 that occurred right here in Maryland," Gilchrest said. "And to learn how close we came to losing our precious independence. This trail will not only teach Americans about the War of 1812, but it will help us remember our forefathers who gave their lives fighting for our freedom."

The state of Maryland, too, has been working to develop its own historic trail based around 1812. Maryland tourism officials are modeling their 1812 trail after the success of the Virginia Civil War Trails program, which promotes historical tourism. Maryland does not have the number of Civil War battlefields that Virginia does, but when it comes to the War of 1812, the state's Chesapeake Bay region is rich in history. Tourism officials hope to tap into this regional history, with Fort McHenry and The Star-Spangled Banner serving as the centerpiece of the trail.

During 1999 and 2000, archaeologists Dwayne Pickett and Keith Heinrich undertook a massive survey of 1812 sites in Maryland. The effort was funded by the National Park Service's American Battlefield Protection Program. This was the most comprehensive and thorough archaeological and historical survey of the War of 1812 ever done in the Chesapeake Bay region. The list of historical sites relating to 1812 was compiled by preservationist Ralph Eshelman. Altogether, he located 338 sites in Maryland, six in Virginia and fifty-one in Washington, D.C. Almost all the sites are centered around the Chesapeake Bay and its tributaries, which underscores the fact that 1812 was an amphibious war closely tied to Royal Navy operations.

The list of sites included five battles—Baltimore, Bladensburg, the first and second battles of St. Leonard's Creek, and Caulk's Field—twenty-four skirmishes, fourty-three raids and three riots, including the "Baltimore Riot" and the "Gin Riot."

Also identified on the list and map were four substantial forts such as Fort McHenry at Baltimore and Fort Washington on the Potomac, forty-eight earthworks that were either entrenchments or gun batteries, and six "booms" or "defensive floating devices" used to block navigation channels that might have been used by the British.

Pickett's role was to investigate the archaeological potential of twenty-three battlefield, skirmish and battery sites. Unfortunately, his findings showed that Maryland's efforts might be a case of too little, too late. As Pickett and

Heinrich pointed out during their work at Elk Landing, precious few sites remain that have not been obliterated or encroached upon by urban growth and development. Only in rural areas such as Cecil County do undisturbed areas exist.

"I found that sixteen sites had been heavily disturbed by construction activities or by collectors," Pickett noted. "Seven sites were archaeologically tested and mapped, of which three yielded artifacts that could be attributed to the War of 1812." Another three sites contained earthworks, but only two of those could be positively identified with the War of 1812, Pickett said.

Troubling, too, was the fact that many of the 1812 sites are in private hands. While private owners have in most cases been good stewards of history, there's no real protection if a private owner chooses to alter the site. Civil War sites are often considered sacred ground that re-enactors and other history buffs will raise millions of dollars to protect, but 1812 sites are ignored.

The survey was a start in terms of calling more attention to the War of 1812. "I think what it is going to do is put Maryland on the map the way the Civil War put Virginia on the map," stated Elise Butler, program director of Preservation Maryland, a non-profit historical preservation association. "We have these great historic sites like Fort McHenry that people go to but don't really know why they are important."

It is possible these attempts at promoting tourism centered around 1812 will increase interest in the war. In any case, it is likely that there will always be someone poking about in this obscure corner of American history.

For a final thought on the War of 1812, turn back to the morning of June 28, 1836. Eighty-five-year-old former president James Madison lay on the day bed in his study at

Montpelier. Nearly sixty years had passed since the signing of the Declaration of Independence. Madison was the last surviving signer. Twenty-one years had elapsed since the end of the Second War of Revolution with England. America was expanding in ways no one could have imagined back in 1776 or even in 1812.

It was obvious to all that the former president was fading away. His niece brought him breakfast, but Madison was unable to eat.

"What is the matter, Uncle James?" she asked.

"Nothing more than a change of mind, my dear," he replied.

Then the aged Founding Father closed his eyes and quietly passed into legend.

The old world of revolution had ended, but a new era in America was just beginning.

Epilogue
What became of the heroes and villains of 1812

Hero has become a shopworn word, the verbal equivalent of blue jeans that have been washed too many times. Local newspapers and TV news are saturated with stories about "everyday heroes" who shovel snowy sidewalks for old ladies or return lost wallets or who do the decent thing by helping someone change a flat tire on a rainy night. It is little wonder that the word seems to fall short when describing Mary Young Pickersgill, Sam Smith and Joshua Barney, just to name a few of the real heroes and heroines of the War of 1812 on Chesapeake Bay.

"Children ought to be learning their names in school because without them it's hard to say how things would have turned out for us," said one 1812 re-enactor.

Every hero shines all the brighter for having a villain to overcome. Anyone who has watched an old western on TV knows that the guys in the black cowboy hats are really there to make the guys in the white hats look good. In the War of 1812, British leaders such as Rear Admiral Sir George Cockburn make perfect villains. Several Americans, due to incompetence that bordered on treason, add to the villainy.

What follows is a list of some heroes and villains from the War of 1812 on Chesapeake Bay, and what became of them in the years after the war. Not included here are James Madison, Francis Scott Key, Mary Young Pickersgill and Kitty Knight, only because their full stories have been told earlier.

Heroes

Joshua Barney. Capable and brave, Commodore Joshua Barney was a leader men were willing to follow into battle. Unfortunately, Barney is not well known beyond the small circle of 1812 history buffs. He was not even listed in my trusty *Funk & Wagnalls New Encyclopedia*, which skips from a treasonous Dutch statesman named Jan van Olden Barneveldt (1547-1619) to the entry for barn owl. Barn owl but no Barney? Talk about an oversight.

Barney was already in his fifties by the time the War of 1812 came along, which made him on the older side for a field commander, especially in the early 1800s when "over the hill" meant anyone past forty. At least one re-enactor described him in these pages as "something of a duffer."

Barney had served in the American navy, fought in the Revolutionary War, and served with the French navy. As a privateer captain in the first six months of the war he captured several British merchant ships worth $1 million. Barney is often depicted as a salty sea captain and a bit rough around the edges. Nonetheless, he was a man who got things done.

If there had been just a few more leaders like Barney on the Chesapeake Bay, it is likely the British would have had a much harder time. Even as one man, Barney did his best to be everywhere at once. He was at St. Leonard's Creek, Bladensburg and even Fort McHenry.

After the war, Barney never quite recovered from the wound he had received at Bladensburg. A lead musket ball remained buried in his thigh, where it caused him painful episodes as it slid back and forth, grating against bones and flesh. He spent a lot of time traveling on horseback, which made the pain even worse.

Portraits of Barney after the war show a man with a youthful face and long white hair flowing over the collar of his uniform. He became one of the naval officers in charge of the port of Baltimore. Restless as ever, he also speculated in land on the Kentucky frontier. He bought 50,000 acres of "forest and meadow" and in 1818 decided to move his family from Maryland to his Kentucky lands. At Brownsville, Pennsylvania, the old mariner bought a boat to float his family to Pittsburgh and then on to their new holdings. Worn out from the trip, he took sick with a bad sore throat. No sooner had he recovered than his old wound began to act up and he suffered from several severe spasms in his leg. He died on December 1, 1818 at age fifty-nine years and six months. Doctors blamed his death on the wound he received defending Washington City in 1814.

Samuel Smith. The city of Baltimore was lucky to have Sam Smith, the competent politician-soldier who led the city in turning back the British attack. He was sixty-three in 1814 when the battle of Baltimore took place but he had another twenty years of public service ahead of him.

Born in Carlisle, Pennsylvania, he was the son of a wealthy merchant who moved to Baltimore when Smith was a young boy. During the Revolution, Smith served at Long Island, Brooklyn Heights, Harlem Plains, White Plains, Brandywine and Monmouth. He survived the winter at Valley Forge. Smith also served as commander of Fort Mifflin on the Delaware River. The fort's strategic hold on the river managed to delay Admiral Howe's fleet for forty days, a situation that contributed to Burgoyne's surrender. It is likely that Smith learned the value of strong defensive position during his command at Fort Mifflin.

Smith foresaw that the British would attack Baltimore in force and he was determined that the city would be able to defend itself. He appointed himself as the city's chief defender and set about rebuilding Fort McHenry at the harbor's entrance. He also prepared the militia to beat off a British attack. This was no small task, considering that Maryland's wartime leaders rarely agreed on how to defend the state.

Smith was a forceful, take-charge individual who was unafraid to bruise a few egos. Not everyone was quick to obey his orders, but he managed to cajole or threaten them into assisting in the defense of Baltimore. He also had a large personal fortune which he pledged toward the city's defense.

His military career did not end with the War of 1812. Smith was called back to service in 1835 at age eighty-three, when Baltimore was overwhelmed by riots brought on by the failure of the Bank of Maryland. With the city mayor recently resigned and Baltimore in flames, old Smith was sworn in as mayor and restored order. He ran the city for three years. He died in 1839 at age eighty-seven.

Considering Smith's considerable achievements, the city he so strongly defended has done little to honor him. No major highways or bridges are named after him. A nine-foot tall statue of Smith stands beside Francis Scott Key Highway in Baltimore. Not many passersby stop to read the inscription.

MAJ. GEN. SAMUEL SMITH
1752-1839
Under his command the attack
of the British upon Baltimore
by land and sea, September 12-14,
1814, was repulsed.
Member of Congress 40 successive years.
President of the United States Senate.
Secretary of the Navy.
Mayor of Baltimore.
Hero of both wars for American Independence.

John Steuart Skinner. Here is a man who has been overshadowed by his famous friend and companion, Francis Scott Key. Skinner, who witnessed the bombardment of Fort McHenry alongside Key, might be the one we remember today if only he had been something of a poet.

It was Michael Smolek at Jefferson-Patterson Park and Museum who first alerted me to Skinner's importance. "Do you know who Francis Scott Key is? How about Dr. Beanes? How about John Steuart Skinner?" Smolek had quizzed me in his office with its distant view of the Patuxent River. "To bring 1812 to popular attention it would take Steven Spielberg making a movie about Joshua Barney or John Steuart Skinner or maybe even Charles Ball." Charles Ball, another overlooked hero of the war in Maryland, was a free African-American who fought with Joshua Barney's flotilla.

After the battle of Baltimore, Skinner read Key's handwritten poem and pronounced that it described "the period of anxiety to all, but never of despair." He took a copy to a local newspaper, *The Baltimore Patriot,* which published the poem the next week. It was the first publication of *The Star-Spangled Banner.* The rest, as they say, is history.

According to Smolek, Skinner was notable for another reason. Born in Calvert County in 1788, he owned a farm along the Patuxent at what is now Jefferson-Patterson Park and the archaeological facility. Smolek speculated that Commodore Barney, seeking a refuge from the British fleet, took his flotilla there at Skinner's suggestion. Skinner's local knowledge might have had something to do with the success of the American flotilla in the sea battle at St. Leonard's Creek. He risked his property and his life to help fight the British.

Skinner went on to become postmaster of Baltimore from 1822 to 1837. From 1844 to 1845 he was assistant postmaster general of the United States. He also was the publisher of several journals, including *The American Farmer.* This quiet patriot died in 1851.

Major George Armistead. When Armistead took command of Fort McHenry on June 27, 1814, he already had an impressive military resume. He had served as second in command at the fort from 1807 to 1812, then fought on the Canadian frontier, where he was promoted to major and took part in the capture of Fort George. Upon returning to take command of Fort McHenry, Armistead wasted no time getting the neglected fort into battle order. He worked closely with General Sam Smith to make sure that Baltimore was properly defended. He also asked Mary Pickersgill to make a huge flag to fly above the fort.

After the American victory, Armistead was near collapse from exhaustion, fever, and the stress of the battle. He temporarily gave up command and crawled into bed for some much-needed sleep. Sadly, historians say Armistead never really recovered from the rigors of commanding Fort McHenry during the British attack. His health suffered and he died in 1818 at age thirty-eight.

Villains

Admiral Sir George Cockburn. He was the man Chesapeake Bay residents hated so much that they put a price of $1,000 on his head. The closest comparison that might be made to Cockburn is General Sherman, who put the state of Georgia to the torch during the Civil War. The South had Sherman—the Chesapeake Bay had Cockburn. No one ever collected the reward and Cockburn eventually went on to a long and distinguished career in the Royal Navy.

Born in 1772, Cockburn was descended from Scottish lords. He went to sea at age nine. The young Cockburn caught the attention of the legendary Admiral Horatio Nelson, who praised the boy's ability.

Cockburn remains such an interesting character. Even Marylanders would have to admit that he was a highly capable commander and brilliant strategist, just the sort of man Americans wished they had on their side in 1812. He understood the advantages of a hit-and-run amphibious campaign and never let himself be bogged down by extended land operations. The furthest he got from his ships while in the Chesapeake region was likely during the attack on Washington, where he rather famously sat down in the empty White House and enjoyed the dinner that had been set out for President Madison.

It is true that Cockburn allowed excesses and brutality. A witness described how British forces under Cockburn ransacked the local church, built in 1736, in the village of Chaptico in St. Mary's County:

I passed through Chaptico shortly after the enemy had left it, and I am sorry to say that their conduct would have disgraced cannibals. . . Will you believe me when I tell you that the sunken graves were converted into barbecue holes? The remaining glass of the church windows broken, the communion table used as a dinner table, and then broken into pieces. Bad as the above may appear, it dwindles into insignificance when compared to what follows: the vault was entered and the remains of the dead disturbed.

These outrages were nothing compared to what happened in Hampton, Virginia, on June 24, 1813. Cockburn's sailors and a force of marines quickly captured the town and occupied it until June 27. The admiral let his men run wild. French soldiers fighting for the British looted homes and raped women. Prisoners were executed out of hand. The cemetery of the Episcopal Church was used as a slaughterhouse for stolen cattle. Anger at what the British had done was so great that "Remember Hampton" became the battle cry of the local militia. Widespread news of the atrocities helped unite Americans against the invaders.

What struck me the most about Cockburn was that after reading several books about the War of 1812, I could not find a single one of his contemporaries who had a positive comment about the man other than to acknowledge his military skills. He may have been a capable naval officer, but many who knew him complained about his overbearing personality.

Lieutenant Colonel Sir Charles Napier, a respected career British army officer who was with Cockburn at Hampton, remarked,

Cockburn's confidence in his luck is the very thing to be feared; it is worse than 1,000 yankees." In addition, Napier did not enjoy carrying out the campaign of terror against Chesapeake Bay residents, claiming, "Strong is my dislike to what is perhaps a necessary part of our job; namely, plundering and ruining the peasantry.

British author C.S. Forester, famed for creating the Horatio Hornblower character that was the hero of several novels about the Royal Navy, made an astute observation about Cockburn's inability to fathom Americans in his book, *The Age of Fighting Sail.* Forester wrote, "He was an able and active officer, but he displayed complete ignorance of the people he was fighting if he expected a Maryland farmer to part with his herd in exchange for bills redeemable in London at some vague future date."

Cockburn also underestimated the Americans and seemed unable to understand why they put up a fight when resistance was futile. He punished the civilian population mercilessly whenever they took up arms against the British. The admiral explained that he ordered homes in Havre de Grace burned, "to cause the proprietors (who had deserted them and formed part of the militia who had fled to the woods) to understand and feel what they were liable to bring upon themselves by building batteries and acting toward us with so much useless rancor."

Americans and Cockburn's fellow British officers were not the only ones who found the admiral to be insufferable. In 1815, Cockburn was ordered to escort Napoleon Bonaparte on the voyage to his island exile on St. Helena. Briefly, he acted as the former emperor's jailer. The emperor described Cockburn as "capricious, choleric, vain and overbearing." Cockburn never let Napoleon forget who ruled St. Helena. The admiral wrote in his journal, "It is clear he is still inclined to act the sovereign occasionally, but I cannot allow it."

Cockburn served as governor of St. Helena in 1815 and 1816, then was promoted to junior lord of the admiralty. He became first sea lord in 1841 and admiral of the fleet in 1851. He died at age eighty-one on August 19, 1853, just a few days short of what would have been the thirty-ninth anniversary of the burning of Washington.

Vice Admiral Sir Alexander Cochrane. Fans of the popular seafaring novels written by the late Patrick O'Brian may know that the character of Jack Aubrey is based on the real-life Alexander Cochrane. Admiral Cochrane had overall command of British sea forces in North America during the War of 1812. Under Cochrane's direction, the scope of the war soon expanded, with raids up the Connecticut River and against Massachusetts ports. Northern Maine was attacked and occupied by the British. Cochrane explained that the excessive brutality sometimes exhibited by his troops was in retaliation for Americans burning government buildings in the Canadian town of York—the present day city of Toronto. Determined to teach Americans a lesson about the cost of defying the British, he ordered Cockburn "to destroy and lay waste such towns and districts upon the coast as you may find assailable."

Cochrane made no secret of his hatred for Americans. He may have been motivated by revenge for his brother's death in 1781 at the Battle of Yorktown. He vowed that the War of 1812 would end when Americans had been "drubbed into good manners."

Cochrane died in 1832.

These last two "villains" of 1812 are actually Americans, but their blatant incompetence leaves little choice but to include them among the bad guys.

Brigadier General William H. Winder. This Baltimore lawyer-turned-soldier oversaw the defense of Maryland against the British invasion in the summer of 1814. Winder's inability to organize his forces led to the United States capital being burned. If it had not been for Sam Smith, it is likely Baltimore would have fallen as well on Winder's watch.

Born in 1775, Winder was a native of Somerset County on Maryland's Eastern Shore. He moved to Baltimore in 1807, where he became a successful lawyer and also an officer of local militia. When war came in 1812, he volunteered to fight and became a brigadier general in the spring of 1813. His military command was cut short when he was captured on

June 6, 1813, during the Great Lakes campaign. Nearly 2,000 Americans were overcome by 750 British soldiers during a night attack when American sentries fell asleep at their posts.

Following that debacle, Winder was briefly held as a prisoner of war. But in the odd and gentlemanly way in which war was conducted in 1812, Winder was paroled and released by the British. He spent the next year traveling between Montreal and Washington, successfully negotiating the end of a serious hostage crisis involving prisoners of war. It was during these negotiations that he met Madison and James Monroe, with whom he became lifelong friends.

Winder was released from his terms of "imprisonment" in July 1814 and the president soon appointed him to oversee the defense of Maryland. His credentials as a general were thin, but Winder was related to Levin Winder, Maryland's Federalist governor. This was a connection President Madison thought would be useful in gaining support for the state's defense.

Things did not go well from the start. Historian Harry Coles describes Winder as a "will-o'-the-wisp commander" in his book on 1812. "From early July until he arrived at Bladensburg on August 24, Winder was a study in unproductive motion."

Theoretically, Winder commanded an army of a few regulars and up to 15,000 militia. The reality was that of the 3,000 militia called up in July only 300 appeared for duty. Most of them did not even have proper weapons, ammunition or food. To make matters worse, Winder was at a loss for what to do with the men once he got them.

Winder tried to get more troops and supplies but his pleas fell on deaf ears. The secretary of war had not seen fit to give Winder any staff, so he was forced to carry messages and run errands himself. He also did his own scouting to get the lay of the land. Winder spent endless hours in the saddle. The day before the battle of Bladensburg, Winder wore out three horses. That night, his senses dulled by exhaustion, he fell into a ditch and injured himself. The battle itself was an embarrassing defeat for the Americans. With the militia swept aside, the British found a clear road to Washington.

An official investigation by Congress and the army into the fiasco that led to the capture of Washington City found no fault with Winder and he remained in the military until he was honorably discharged in June 1815. He resumed his law practice in Baltimore, served in the state legislature, and died on May 24, 1824 at age forty-nine.

John Armstrong. President Madison named Armstrong to his cabinet on June 14, 1813. Armstrong had served as minister to France but the appointment was really an attempt by Madison to build political alliances. Armstrong was a force in New York politics, and with so much military action taking place along the border with Canada, Madison needed that state firmly in his camp. Armstrong would prove to be a disastrous choice for secretary of war.

Simple incompetence on Armstrong's part might have been forgivable, but he deliberately ignored his duties at times in an attempt to undermine the Madison administration. Armstrong believed that making the president look bad would help his own chances of occupying the White House. This strategy ultimately led to the White House being burned by the British invaders.

Armstrong's shortcomings were described by at least one acquaintance as "obstinacy and self-conceit." He was the author of a popular book published in 1814 entitled, *Hints to Young Generals.* Instead of putting his name on the book—it was no secret he was the author—it claimed rather cutely to have been written "By an Old Soldier." The book sold well, pleasing the secretary of war, who bragged to his wife that the writing of it occupied him for no more than three or four days.

If only he had followed his own advice about soldiering. He stubbornly refused to do anything to defend the United States. When residents of St. Mary's County pleaded for help in the face of several British raids, Armstrong replied, "It cannot be expected that I can defend every man's turnip patch." When a desperate General Winder begged for more help, Armstrong told him the defense of the capital was a "local problem" that the militia general would have to resolve himself. Chesapeake Bay residents were on their own.

Even when it became obvious that the British intended to attack Washington, Armstrong remained in denial. Just days before the invasion, when President Madison reprimanded him for not doing enough to defend the capital, a sulky Armstrong reacted by doing even less. He sent important dispatches to Winder through the regular mail rather than by courier.

After the burning of Washington, the famously even-tempered President Madison finally lost his patience with Armstrong and suggested a "temporary retirement." Armstrong resigned on September 4, 1814, only days before the attack on Baltimore. James Monroe took over operation of the war department in addition to his duties as secretary of state.

Armstrong's handling of the crisis in August 1814 ended his political career. He retired to his home in Red Hook, New York, and died there on April 1, 1843.

The Star-Spangled Banner

Oh, say can you see by the dawn's early light
What so proudly we hailed at the twilight's last gleaming?
Whose broad stripes and bright stars thru the perilous fight,
O'er the ramparts we watched were so gallantly streaming?
And the rocket's red glare, the bombs bursting in air,
Gave proof thru the night that our flag was still there.
Oh, say does that star-spangled banner yet wave
O'er the land of the free and the home of the brave?

On the shore, dimly seen through the mists of the deep,
Where the foe's haughty host in dread silence reposes,
What is that which the breeze, o'er the towering steep,
As it fitfully blows, half conceals, half discloses?
Now it catches the gleam of the morning's first beam,
In full glory reflected now shines in the stream;
'Tis the star-spangled banner! Oh long may it wave
O'er the land of the free and the home of the brave.

And where is that band who so vauntingly swore
That the havoc of war and the battle's confusion,
A home and a country should leave us no more!
Their blood has washed out of their foul footsteps' pollution.
No refuge could save the hireling and slave
From the terror of flight and the gloom of the grave:
And the star-spangled banner in triumph doth wave
O'er the land of the free and the home of the brave.

Oh! thus be it ever, when freemen shall stand
Between their loved home and the war's desolation!
Blest with victory and peace, may the heav'n rescued land
Praise the Power that hath made and preserved us a nation.
Then conquer we must, when our cause it is just,
And this be our motto: "In God is our trust."
And the star-spangled banner in triumph shall wave
O'er the land of the free and the home of the brave.
— Francis Scott Key

An 1812 Timeline

1783 War of Independence ends

1793-1815 War between Britain and France

1806 Battle on Chesapeake Bay between *HMS Leopard* and *USS Chesapeake*

1809 President James Madison takes office

1812 Madison re-elected by taking pro-war stance

June 18, 1812 United States declares war

Summer 1812 U.S. forces invade Canada and suffer embarrassing defeats

March 3, 1813 Admiral George Cockburn arrives on Chesapeake Bay

April 29, 1813 Frenchtown burned

April 29, 1813 Militia turns back British marines in Battle of Elkton

May 3, 1813 Havre de Grace burned; Principio Furnace burned

May 6, 1813 Georgetown and Fredericktown burned

Aug. 10, 1813 Mary Young Pickersgill completes the Star-Spangled Banner flag

Oct. 5, 1813 British ally and Shawnee leader Tecumseh killed at Battle of Thames in Canada, ending American Indian hopes of stopping westward expansion by United States

Feb. 26, 1814 Baltimore privateer Chasseur defeats *HMS St. Lawrence* off Cuba

June 7, 1814 First Battle of St. Leonard's Creek

June 26, 1814 Second Battle of St. Leonard's Creek

Aug. 24-25, 1814 Battle of Bladensburg; Washington captured and burned

Aug. 26, 1814 Village of Brookeville becomes United States capital for a day

Aug. 31, 1814 Battle of Caulk's Field and battlefield death of Sir Peter Parker

Sept. 11, 1814 Battle of Plattsburg Bay puts Great Lakes firmly in U.S. control

Sept. 12-14, 1814 Battle of Baltimore

Dec. 24, 1814 Treaty of Ghent signed in Belgium ends War of 1812

Jan. 8, 1815 Battle of New Orleans

Feb. 16, 1815 Senate ratifies Treaty of Ghent; peace official

1817 James Madison ends second term at president

1828 Andrew Jackson, hero of New Orleans, elected president

June 28, 1836 Former president Madison dies at Montpelier

Nov. 22, 1855 Death of Miss Kitty Knight, 1812 heroine of Georgetown

April 12, 1861 Civil War begins; Fort McHenry soon becomes prison for Confederates

Jan. 1, 1863 Abraham Lincoln issues Emancipation Proclamation, freeing slaves in Southern states

December 1865 Last remaining slaves freed in Delaware and Kentucky, eight months after end of Civil War

1905 Death of Hiram Cronk, last surviving veteran of the War of 1812

1925 Fort McHenry declared national park

1931 *The Star-Spangled Banner* becomes official national anthem by act of Congress

1936 Death of last-known widow of a War of 1812 veteran

1961 War of 1812's "Uncle Sam" becomes official national mascot

October 1999 Wreckage of ship burned by British found at Frenchtown

1999 Congressman Wayne T. Gilchrest urges creation of an 1812 history trail in Maryland

1999 Historic Elk Landing Foundation established; work begins to restore Fort Hollingsworth that defended against British in 1813

2004 Baltimore Mayor Martin O'Malley asks that the city adopt the fifteen-star, fifteen-stripe flag from the War of 1812

2005 Restoration work continues on original Star-Spangled Banner flag

2012 Bicentennial of America's Second War of Revolution

Bibliography

Barney, Mary. *A Biographical Memoir of the Late Commodore Joshua Barney.* Boston: Gray and Bowen, 1832.

Calkins, Carroll C., editor. *The Story of America.* Pleasantville, New York: Reader's Digest Association, Inc., 1975.

Coles, Harry L. *The War of 1812.* Chicago: The University of Chicago Press, 1965.

Crownfield, Gertrude. *Conquering Kitty: A Romance of the Sassafras River.* Philadelphia: J.B. Lippincott Co., 1935.

Dupuy, George, editor. *The Harper Encyclopedia of Military Biography.* New York: Harper Collins, 1992.

Filby, P.W. and Edward G. Howard, editors. *Star-Spangled Books: Books, Sheet Music, Newspapers, Manuscripts and Persons Associated With "The Star-Spangled Banner."* Baltimore: The Maryland Historical Society, 1972.

George, Christopher T. *Terror on the Chesapeake: The War of 1812 on the Bay.* Shippensburg, Pennsylvania: White Mane Books, 2000.

George, James L. *History of Warships: From Ancient Times to the Twenty-First Century.* Annapolis, Maryland: Naval Institute Press, 1998.

Forester, C.S. *The Age of Fighting Sail.* Garden City, New York: Doubleday & Company Inc., 1956.

Leech, Margaret. *Reveille in Washington 1860-1865.* New York: Carroll & Graf Publishers, Inc. 1986.

The James Madison Center at James Madison University *www.jmu.edu/madison/center/index.htm*

Molotsky, Irvin. *The Flag, the Poet & the Song: The story of the Star-Spangled Banner.* New York: Dutton, 2001.

Muller, Charles G. *The Darkest Day: 1814 The Washington-Baltimore Campaign.* Philadelphia: J.B. Lippincott Co., 1963.

Nevin, David. *1812.* New York: Forge 1996.

Paine, Ralph D. *Joshua Barney: A Forgotten Hero of Blue Water.* New York: The Century Company, 1924.

Pitch, Anthony S. *The Burning of Washington: The British Invasion of 1814.* Annapolis, Maryland: Naval Institute Press, 1998.

Pride of Baltimore, Inc. *www.pride2.org*

Remini, Robert V. *The Battle of New Orleans: Andrew Jackson and America's First Military Victory.* New York: Viking, 1999.

Rutland, Robert Allen. *The Presidency of James Madison.* University Press of Kansas, 1990.

Sheads, Scott. *Fort McHenry.* Baltimore: The Nautical & Aviation Publishing Company of America, 1995.

Shomette, Donald G. *Lost Towns of Tidewater Maryland.* Centreville, Maryland: Tidewater Publishers, 2000.

Van Doren, Charles, editor. *Webster's American Biographies.* Springfield, Massachusetts: Merriam-Webster, Inc., 1984.

Whitehorne, Joseph W.A. *The Battle for Baltimore 1814.* Baltimore: The Nautical & Aviation Publishing Company of America, 1997.

About the Author

David Healey was born in Baltimore and developed an interest in history while growing up on a Maryland farm visited by J.E.B. Stuart's cavalry on the road to Gettysburg in 1863. A graduate of Washington College, he works as a newspaper editor. He has written articles on historical topics for *American History*, *The Washington Times* and *Blue & Gray*. He is also the author of three Civil War novels. He lives with his wife and two children along the Chesapeake and Delaware Canal in Cecil County, Maryland. Visit him online at www.davidhealey.net

Printed in the United States
33314LVS00002B/169-189